THE PROPHET OF THE MYRTLE GROVE

THE PROPHET OF THE MYRTLE GROVE

An Exposition of the Prophecy of Zechariah

BY
FREDK. A. TATFORD, LITT. D.

Henry E. Walter Ltd.
&
Prophetic Witness Movement
International

First published 1971

0 85479 570 7

Henry E. Walter Ltd, 26 Grafton Road, Worthing
&
Prophetic Witness Movement International,
2 Upperton Gardens, Eastbourne

Printed by Cox & Wyman Ltd,
London, Fakenham and Reading

Preface

The last three of the Minor Prophets seem to have a particular relevance to the present day. On the horizon they could see the indications that the Eternal was about to break into time. The details were not clear and the difference between the First Advent and the Second Advent was not plainly disclosed: but it was plain that climactic events were about to happen. That is also the position today. Life's uncertainties, economic instability, industrial unrest, political weakness, universal lack of leadership – all emphasize the necessity for a Divine intervention. We seem to be on the brink of some other climactic event. *We are!* The return of the Saviour for His Church is almost here. The signs accumulate: the only question is, When?

Zechariah has his message for days like ours. During the last few years the author has given quite a number of lectures and Bible readings on the Book, and has been urged repeatedly to put them into print. The lectures have now been expanded into book form in answer to such requests, and it is hoped that the following pages may prove of interest and help to some.

FREDK. A. TATFORD

Acknowledgements

We gratefully acknowledge permission from Zondervan Publishing House, Grand Rapids, to make a number of quotations from 'Commentary on Zechariah' by Merrill F. Unger. These are indicated in the text.

Contents

Foreword

There have been periods in the history of the Christian Church when the study of Biblical prophecy has attracted scant attention. The relevance of such themes to the contemporary situation was scarcely apparent. It is a cause for rejoicing that ours is an age in which eschatology has come into its own on the theological scene. Never have the doctrines of the end been accorded more prominence. Whilst it is true that traditional interpretations have been subjected to radical criticism in recent years, the fundamental significance of prophecy is nevertheless increasingly recognized. As Professor John Macquarrie has put it, 'eschatology is the element that introduces perspective into the Christian theological picture.' That perspective is being restored today.

Such being the case, there is a continuing demand for careful, detailed expositions of Biblical prophecies, and it is for this reason that Dr. Tatford's treatment of Zechariah is to be welcomed. He writes, as is to be expected, from a convinced premillennialist position, but throughout his commentary he is at pains to make his point with discretion and in charity. His method is comprehensive and his style so compelling that a wide range of readership will be reached. What he offers will form an admirable introduction to Zechariah for any who have not yet seriously studied the book, whilst even those most familiar with it will find much to inform and stimulate.

Martin Luther, the pioneer Protestant Reformer, described Zechariah as the quintessence of the prophets. We may well agree with him in regarding it as a refined extract of the prophetic genre. It is a superlative example of this particular form of revelation, and affords a link which supplies coherence to the entire scheme of scriptural prediction. Zechariah ought to be prescribed reading for all who would master prophetic truth. What follows in these pages will provide an invaluable clue to the understanding of the prophet's message.

A. SKEVINGTON WOOD

Cliff Cottage

CHAPTER 1

The Author and His Book

Relatively little is known of the three post-exilic prophets, of whom Zechariah was the second, but, unlike Haggai and Malachi, minimal details are at least given of his genealogy. The name he bore, which means 'God remembers', was that of more than twenty other persons in the Old Testament. He is personally described as the son of Berechiah (whose name meant 'God blesses') and the grandson of Iddo (the significance of whose name was 'the appointed time'). Ezra 5:1 and Neh. 12:16 refer to him as the son of Iddo, from which it may be deduced that his father Berechiah died while Zechariah was still young and prior to the death of Iddo and therefore before he could become the head of the family. The prophet was apparently born in Babylon during the exile and he evidently accompanied his grandfather on the return to Palestine of the first caravan under Zerubbabel in 536 B.C. (Neh. 12:4). Iddo was the head of one of the twelve priestly courses instituted by David and Solomon (1 Chron. 23:6; 2 Chron. 8:14), and Zechariah presumably succeeded him in this office some time after the return, although there is no specific indication of when this occurred in the book which bears his name. (There is possibly an implication of this in Neh. 12:16). He was, in any case, a priest as well as a prophet.

It is fairly clear that Zechariah was called to the prophetic office at a comparatively early age. As David Baron says in *The Visions and Prophecies of Zechariah* (p. 7), 'That he was scarcely a full-grown man may be inferred from the fact that in chapter 2:4 he is addressed as *naar* (i.e. boy, lad or youth)' – the same word as was used of David by Saul in 1 Sam. 17:38. He is said, however, to have still been active in the days of Nehemiah, somewhere about 455 to 433 B.C. and consequently to have lived to be over 100 years old.

He was not identical with the Zechariah to whom our Lord referred in Matt. 23:35, and who was there described as the son of Berechiah and as having been slain between the temple and the altar. An earlier Zechariah, who was the son of Jehoiada, was stoned to death in the court of the temple in the reign of Joash (2 Chron. 24:20, 21) and our Lord's allusion was almost undoubtedly to that Zechariah and not to the author of the Old Testament book. Since the corresponding record in Luke 11:51 omits any mention of Berechiah, it is possible that the Master did not, in fact, quote any patronymic and that the name of Berechiah was interpolated in error at a later date. It is reasonably clear that the Zechariah referred to in the gospel narratives was the son of Jehoiada and not of Berechiah. Josephus mentions the assassination in the temple of another Zechariah, who was the son of Baruch, but this happened in A.D. 68 and could not, therefore, have been the incident to which our Lord referred. So far as is known, Iddo's grandson died peacefully and naturally and did not suffer martyrdom for his faith in God.

Certain traditions regarding his life and ministry do exist but, as one writer pertinently remarks, 'The patristic notices of the prophet are worth nothing. According to these, he exercised his prophetic office in Chaldea, and wrought many miracles there; returned to Jerusalem at an advanced age, where he discharged the duties of the priesthood, and where he died, and was buried by the side of Haggai.' There is, however, no support for these stories, either in secular history or in the Biblical records. Certainly, on the Mount of Olives, there is a catacomb which was used by early Christians as a burial place and which is also venerated by the Jews as the tomb of the prophets Haggai, Zechariah and Malachi, but confirmation of this traditional site of Zechariah's grave is lacking. (To the west of this and south of Absalom's Pillar along the valley of the Kidron is the alleged tomb of the Zechariah of Matt. 23:35.)

According to Jewish tradition, Zechariah was a member of the Great Synagogue, of which Ezra was the president, but if, as is generally supposed this council (which had 120 members and was succeeded by the Sanhedrin) was first organized by Nehemiah between 400 and 410 B.C., it would have been wellnigh impossible chronologically for the prophet to have been a member. It is alleged that he participated in the preparation of the liturgical service for the restored temple, and that he also took part in the compilation of the canon of the Old Testament: these claims may very well have some substance in them, although there is no definite confirmation available. The Septuagint credits him furthermore with the authorship of Ps. 137 and 138 and, jointly with Haggai, of Ps. 145, 146, 147 and 148, although it must be acknowledged that Ps. 138 and 145 are commonly attributed to David.

The date of the Book of Zechariah is made clear in the opening verse – it was the eighth month in the second year of Darius Hystaspes, i.e. about 520 B.C. Not all of the book was penned at this time: in fact, there seems to have been a considerable lapse of time between the conclusion of chapter 8 and the commencement of chapter 9. The first eight chapters contain a number of references to the prophet by name and the chapters so cohere that no question has ever been raised regarding their Zecharian authorship. Chapters 9 to 14, which, it is generally concluded, were penned at a much later date than the first half of the book, make no mention of the prophet by name. The style of these later chapters is more lively and imaginative than the plain and prosaic record of the visions of the earlier chapters, and it has also been argued that there is even a different religious attitude: as one German writer puts it, 'One who denies salvation to the Samaritans as harshly as Zechariah did in chapters 5, 7, 8, certainly cannot, a few years later, include these Samaritans in his promises of salvation, chapters 9, 10', but this argument is somewhat fallacious – the alleged exclusion in the earlier passages is not so definite as implied and the argument also takes no account of the grace of God. The difference in style may be attributable partly to the different content and partly to the difference in age of the prophet. Some critics have maintained that the reference to the Ionian Greeks (Javan) in Zech. 9:13 necessitates a much later date for that section of the book than is normally allocated to it, but Greece was in existence well within Zechariah's day and Jewish captives had been sold as slaves by her (Joel 3:6; Obad. 20). Despite the case which is sometimes made out for a second author to chapters 9 to 14, there are many internal evidences to support the view that the whole of the book is by one author.

For over two thousand years the whole of the book was, in fact, recognized universally as the work of Zechariah, and it was included in its entirety in the Old Testament canon. It was not until 1644 that Hugo Grotius questioned the Zecharian authorship of chapters 9 to 14, and in 1653 Joseph Mede (*Works*, pp. 786, 833) suggested that these chapters were the work of Jeremiah. Mede used the arguments, *inter alia*, of the irreconcilability of Matt. 27:9 with a Zecharian authorship of Zech. 11:12, 13, and also the differences in style employed. The arguments for and against the unity of the book and the common authorship of the whole have been set out briefly by J. S. Wright in *The New Bible Dictionary* (p. 1356) and more fully by W. A. Wright in W. Smith's *Dictionary of the Bible* (pp. 1825–1833) and by Sir George Adam Smith in *The Book of the Twelve Prophets* (pp. 450 – 455), and they have been repeated (in some cases almost verbatim) in later works and there seems no point in repeating them once more. It is perhaps pertinent to point out that the canon of the Old Testament was completed in the third century B.C. (Josephus indicates that the historical books had been completed in the fifth century) and, as one writer remarks, 'its compilers had abundant opportunity to satisfy themselves as to the claims of the different classes of writings upon which they adjudicated'. If tradition is correct in its assertion (which cannot be confirmed) that Zechariah played a prominent part with Ezra in the compilation of the Old Testament canon, it is extremely unlikely that he would have concurred in the words of some anonymous prophet being added to his writings or represented as an integral part of them. It is also relevant that the references by the Master to 'all the prophets' in Luke 24:25, 27 would have covered the Book of Zechariah as a whole and, therefore, virtually constitute an imprimatur upon it by our Lord. The testimony of the Jews regarding the unity of the book is unanimous. As T. W. Chambers writes in Lange's *Commentary on the Minor Prophets* (p. 15), 'Not only the learned scribes in the days of Ezra and afterwards who compiled the canon, but the schools of Hillel and Shammai who flourished in Jerusalem just before and after the time of our Lord, the great Jewish seminaries of Tiberias and Babylon, the authors of the Targums, and the continuous series of learned rabbis down to the Reformation, all with one consent, accept the Book of Zechariah, just as it stands in the Old Testament, as the product of one man, the contemporary of Haggai and Zerubbabel.'

The character and composition of the book reflect to some extent the prophet's early upbringing. 'His birth and early education in Babylon,' says T. T. Perowne (*Haggai and Zechariah*, p. 48), 'account for his frequent use, in common with Ezekiel and Daniel, of visions and allegories; the Divine Spirit adapting Himself, as ever, to the capacity and training of the human instrument, in imparting His revelations.' Perowne considers that Zechariah's visions, in fact, are tinged with Persian imagery. In *The Jewish Church* (vol. III, p. 102) Stanley remarks, 'He saw the earth, as it now presented itself to the enlarged vision of those who had listened to the wise men of Chaldea, its four corners growing into the four horns that toss and gore the lesser powers of the world (1:18, 19); the celestial messengers riding on horses, red or dappled, hurrying through the myrtle groves that then clothed the base of Olivet, or from the four quarters of the heavens driving in chariots, each with its coloured horses, to and fro, across the Persian empire (1:8–11; 6:1–8), as in the vast machinery of the posts for which it was celebrated, and bringing back the tidings of war and peace.' But the book has always been regarded as difficult of interpretation. The Jewish commentator, Solomon Ben Jarchi (usually referred to as Rashi) for instance, says, 'The prophecy is very dark, for it contains visions much like dreams, which want interpreting, and we will never succeed in finding the true meaning until the Teacher of righteousness arrives.' To the Christian, with the later revelation of the New Testament and particularly of its closing book, there is perhaps greater light now than in an earlier day.

Zechariah's inspired utterances were concerned, in the first instance, with the declension of his people and the need to encourage them in the rebuilding of the temple, although, of course, the implications of his statements were far deeper and more far-reaching than the immediate circumstances. An appreciation of the historical background is, however, essential if the significance of the book is to be plain.

When Nebuchadnezzar captured Jerusalem in 598 B.C., he spoiled the city and the temple and deported all but the poorest of Judah (2 Kings 24:11–16). Nine years later, in consequence of the rebellion of the puppet king Zedekiah, the Babylonians destroyed Jerusalem and carried away captive the remainder of the people (2 Kings 24:20 to 25:8–11). After Cyrus had added Babylon to the Persian Empire, however, he issued a decree in 536 B.C., authorizing the exiled Jews to return to their own country and to rebuild the temple (Ezra 1:1–4). A large company (estimated by Perowne to consist of 42,360 men and some 200,000 free persons – men, women and children – together with 7,327 male and female slaves – see Ezra 2) accordingly set out for their own land under the leadership of Joshua and Zerubbabel, and it was not long before they had laid the foundation of the sacred building. But the construction of the temple was hampered and frustrated by the opposition and intrigues of the surrounding nations, and eventually the discouraged Jews, forbidden by the Persian ruler to rebuild the city, gave up the temple work in despair (Ezra 4:21–24). For fifteen years it was left untouched, while the people devoted themselves to their own affairs and to the building of their own houses. At this stage, Haggai was called upon to prophesy to them. His words stirred the nation and shook the people out of their lethargy and despondency, converting them once more into zealous workers for God and His temple. The emperor's own approval was subsequently given and, in less than four years, the rebuilding of the temple was completed (Ezra 6:1–15).

Two months after Haggai's first message and only a few weeks after the Jews had recommenced the building of the temple, Zechariah was Divinely directed to confirm and supplement the message of the other prophet. He accordingly started to prophesy in November 520 B.C., between the second and the third messages of Haggai, but his utterances were by no means as simple and uncomplicated as those of the latter. To quote T. W. Chambers again (op. cit., p. 7), 'His utterances take in the whole character and condition of the remnant people, their present dangers and discouragements, their tendencies to formalism and self-deception, their relations to the surrounding heathen and their influence upon the future prospects of the world. His historical position in the second to fourth years of Darius merely furnishes the background of the delineations he presents of the present and coming fortunes of the kingdom of God.' He looked beyond the present, however, to the ultimate future and he glimpsed the glory of the Second Advent of the Messiah. We also stand in a day of sloth and lethargy, disillusionment and discouragement, with a realization – as Zechariah must have had – that a crisis is imminent and that some climactic event must inevitably burst upon us in the near future. The inspired messages of the prophet so long ago still have their significance for the present day and are perhaps more pertinent now than they have ever been in the past. Zechariah anticipated the first advent of Christ and also His ultimate return to earth. We look into the heavens as we await the first stage of His second advent – His descent to the air to call away His Church.

Zechariah's book may be analysed quite simply as shown below.

Part 1 (Chapters 1 to 8)

1. *Introduction* (1:1–6).
   (*a*) Date and authorship (1:1).
   (*b*) Call to repentance (1:2–6).
2. *Eight Visions* (1:7 to 6:6).
   (*a*) The horsemen in the myrtle grove (1:7–17).
   (*b*) The four horns and four artificers (1:18–21).
   (*c*) Measurement of Jerusalem's ground plan (2:1–13).
   (*d*) The cleansing of the high priest (3:1–10).
   (*e*) The lampstand and olive trees (4:1–14).
   (*f*) The flying roll (5:1–4).
   (*g*) The woman in the ephah (5:5–11).
   (*h*) The chariots of judgement (6:1–8).
3. *Crowning of Joshua* (6:9–15).
4. *Observance of Fasts* (7 and 8).

Part 2 (Chapters 9 to 14)

5. *First Burden* (9–11).
   (*a*) The coming of the King (9 and 10).
   (*b*) Rejection of the Shepherd (11).
6. *Second Burden* (12–14).
   (*a*) Gentile invasion of Israel (12 and 13).
   (*b*) The return in glory (14).

CHAPTER 2

A Call to Repentance

It was the common practice for the Jews to date all events by reference to the years of the reigns of their kings, e.g. Jeremiah declared that the Divine message came to him in the thirteenth year of the reign of Josiah, the king of Judah (Jer. 1:2). Unlike the pre-exilic prophets, Zechariah could not use this method of dating his prophecy, because the throne of Israel and Judah had now no rightful occupant. Instead, he related his ministry – as Haggai had done earlier – to the reign of the heathen Darius (i.e. Darius Hystaspes), thereby emphasizing the fact that the chosen people were without their own sovereign and were subject to the rule of a Gentile power. When God bestowed upon Nebuchadnezzar potential authority over the whole earth (Dan. 2:37, 38), He disclosed that Gentile supremacy would continue until the establishment of a theocratic kingdom on earth (Dan. 2:44, 45). Our Lord subsequently revealed that Israel's misfortunes would continue until the completion of the period of 'the times of the Gentiles' at the coming of the Son of Man (Luke 21:24–27). If the two parts of the Book of Zechariah are from the pen of the same author, the prophecy spans in its scope practically the entire period of 'the times of the Gentiles' and anticipates the succeeding one of the millennium. 'The times of the Gentiles,' writes Dr. H. Grattan Guinness in *Light for the Last Days*, 'are marked by Jewish loss of dominion and independence, by Jewish subjection to and suffering under Gentile conquerors, by the dispersion of the twelve tribes of Israel, and by the subjection of their land.' (See also pp. 30–32 of *God's Programme of the Ages*, by F. A. Tatford.)

Cyrus, the Persian ruler who had authorized the return of the exiles, was succeeded in 529 B.C. by Cambyses. On the latter's death, Darius Hystaspes became emperor of Persia in 521 B.C. and proved himself an outstanding administrator. It is this Darius by whose reign the prophets Haggai and Zechariah dated their messages. In his *Handbook of Biblical Chronology* (pp. 212–213), J. Finegan shows that the second regnal year of

Darius was 520–519 B.C. and that Zechariah's first address was given in October – November, 520 B.C.

The exordium to Zechariah's book was relatively brief but, as M. F. Unger remarks in his *Commentary on Zechariah* (p. 20), 'Its theme strikes the keynote of the entire book and forms an indispensable introduction to it. The truth that it enunciates is one which runs throughout the revealed ways of God with man; namely, the appropriation and enjoyment of God's promises of blessing must be perfected by genuine repentance. . . . Although the immutability of God's Word and the continuity of His plans for Israel assure the fulfilment of these purposes, nevertheless the people are not to divorce divine grace from human responsibility.' This is a lesson which should still be conned today. Communion with God is dependent upon spiritual condition and the deliberate eschewing of all that might dishonour Him.

The introduction to the book ran as follows:

'In the eighth month, in the second year of Darius, the word of Jehovah came to the prophet Zechariah, the son of Berechiah, the son of Iddo, saying, Jehovah was very angry with your fathers. Therefore, say to them, Thus says Jehovah of hosts, Return to me, says Jehovah of hosts, and I will return to you, says Jehovah of hosts. Be not like your fathers, to whom the former prophets cried, Thus says Jehovah of hosts, Return, I beseech you from your evil ways and from your evil deeds. But they did not hear or heed me, says Jehovah. Your fathers, where are they? And the prophets, do they live for ever? But my words and my statutes, which I commanded my servants the prophets. did they not overtake your fathers? So they turned and said, As Jehovah of hosts purposed to deal with us, according to our ways, and according to our deeds, so has He dealt with us' (1:1 – 6).

Zechariah's opening words were arresting. As Wordsworth says, he 'comes forth like John the Baptist, and begins his preaching with a call to repentance, and warns the people by the history of their fathers, that no spiritual privileges will profit them without holiness, but rather will aggravate their guilt and increase their condemnation if they disobey God'. Verses 2 to 6 are possibly only a synopsis of a complete sermon on repentance delivered by the prophet, but their blunt statements and direct appeal certainly contain all the essentials required to touch the conscience of a people already aroused by the words of the contemporaneous prophet, Haggai.

A month earlier, Haggai had envisioned the filling of the millennial temple with the shekinah glory, and a month after Zechariah's first message, had emphasized the effect of the people's uncleanness (Hag. 2:1–14). Zechariah now pleaded for the repentance of the returned exiles. Pressel considers that verse 2 ('Jehovah was very angry with your fathers') was intended as an introductory word to the prophet himself and that it was indicative of the internal pressure under which he entered upon his prophetic ministry. 'A due sense of the power of God's wrath lies at the basis of all true earnestness on the part of the prophets,' he writes, 'imparts its own vehemence to the message, and produces corresponding conviction in them that hear.' Whether or not his restriction of the application of the verse is completely justified, his point is certainly pertinent. It is this vivid realization of the awfulness of the Divine wrath and the dreadfulness of alienation from God, that is so conspicuously missing from the emasculated preaching of the present day. The preachers of another age were far more conscious of its significance. In *Grace Abounding*, John Bunyan, for example, declares that, in his preaching, 'the terrors of the law and guilt for my transgressions lay heavy on my conscience; I preached what I felt, what I smartingly did feel, even that under which my poor soul did groan and tremble to astonishment. Indeed, I have been as one sent unto them from the dead! I went myself in chains, to preach to them in chains; and carried that fire in my own conscience that I persuaded them to be aware of.'

The prophet described God as 'Jehovah Sabaoth' or 'the Lord of hosts'. Jehovah was the name of the eternally existent God of Israel. The word Sabaoth disclosed His supreme authority in every realm, and the name was translated in the Septuagint as 'Ruler of all things'. W. E. Barnes (*Cambridge Bible*, p. xxiv) sees the title as portraying God's 'filling all the universe and possessing all the power and authority ascribed by the heathen to the heavenly bodies. . . . The chariots of Jehovah go through the whole earth, like the messengers of a king, and the Lord Himself decides the fate both of Jerusalem and of the nations which oppress her.' He is the supreme governor, not only over Israel, but over all the nations of the world and His armies stand waiting His behest.

Earlier prophets had repeatedly besought the previous generation of the people to desert their evil ways and deeds, and to turn in repentance to God (e.g. Isa. 55:6, 7; Jer. 3:12, 13; Hos. 7:10; Joel 2:12, 13; Amos 5:4–6), and had warned them of the consequences of their refusal to do so. But they had obdurately persisted in their course, blinded by their depravity to a sense of their sinfulness, and had declined to listen to God's words. Yet His statements were clear and explicit. 'Jehovah has sent to you all his servants the prophets, rising early and sending them; but you have not listened nor inclined your ear to hear,' said Jeremiah. The prophets said, 'Turn you again now, every one of you, from his evil way and from the evil of your doings . . . and go not after other gods to serve them. . . . Yet you have not listened to me, says Jehovah, that you might provoke me to anger with the works of your hands to your own harm' (Jer. 25:4–7; c.f. 35:14–17; 18:11, 12). The Divine pleas were reiterated through prophet after prophet in tones of compassion and warning (Isa. 31:6; Hos. 14:1), but the rebellious nation refused to listen. Ultimately, the long-threatened judgement (Exod. 20:5; Lev. 26:14 ff.; Deut. 28:15–68) fell upon the recusant people and they suffered the penalty of seven decades of captivity. It is insensate folly to imagine that the long-suffering of God implies a condonation of sin. His justice demands the punishment of offences.

Zechariah begged the returned exiles not to repeat the wilful folly of their predecessors. Where were their fathers now? T. V. Moore writes in his book on *Zechariah* (p. 42), 'Once they ruled and worshipped' as their descendants now did. 'The song of the Levite rang through the arches of the temple, the smoke of the victim ascended from its altars, their banner waved over these hills, and their armies struck terror into the hearts of their enemies. But where are they now? Some lie in slaughtered heaps, when the banner of Judah was trampled in the dust, and her bravest sons cut down like grass before the mower's scythe, by the fierce cohorts of the Assyrian. Some lie buried in the ruins of the holy city which they sought to defend from the spoiler. Some are sleeping by the flashing waters of the Euphrates, far from the graves of their fathers, after weeping out a weary life beneath the willows that bend in the land of the stranger.' Where are they now? They might have enjoyed Divine clemency had they turned to God when He appealed to them, but now, because of their deliberate intransigence, they were dead. They had turned a deaf ear to the remonstrances of the earlier prophets and, like the prairie wolf, which swiftly pursued and eventually overtook the fearful traveller, God's sore displeasure had relentlessly followed and overtaken them.

If their fathers had perished, did the prophets themselves live for ever? If the words were a rhetorical question of Zechariah's, the intention was presumably to stress the brevity of life and of the opportunity to repent. The sinners who had been warned, and the prophets who had been the vehicles of that warning, had alike passed off the scene, and the opportunity to respond in penitence had gone for ever for those who had died. Surely the present generation should realize the seriousness and the ominous character of the warning. C. F. Keil (*Commentary on the Minor Prophets*), however, suggests that, in reply to the prophet's question, 'Where are your fathers?' the people had impudently flung it back in the retort, 'And do the prophets live for ever?' In other words, they regarded the question as irrelevant. If God had judged their fathers and had punished them with death, might it not be logically assumed that the prophets had been deemed equally culpable, since they had met with the same fate? Although this is a possible interpretation, it is more probable that both questions were asked by Zechariah and that the implication of his words was that the impenitent, to whom the prophets had spoken, had perished, and that even the prophets, who had borne the message of monition, had also died, but that the Word of God still lived, and was only rendered more emphatic by the experience of those who had refused to hear it. In view of this, Zechariah pleaded, 'Do not be like your fathers'.

The words are even more pertinent today for, as Reinhold Niebuhr said in *Europe's Catastrophe and the Christian Faith* (p. 35), 'the New Testament invariably pictures human history as moving towards a climax in which evil becomes more naked and unashamed, pride more arrogant, and conflict more overt'. The lessons of the past seem to carry no weight. Yet, as D. E. Hart-Davis declared in *The Severity of God* (pp. 104 and 108), 'the judgements of God are continually in operation,' not only in a general sense, but in the particular. 'There is a law operating without cessation in our bodily constitution, and judgement proceeds according as we obey or disobey. The dipsomaniac, the drug addict, the inveterate sensualist, soon begin to manifest the operation of the law that the wages of sin is disease and premature decay. What is true in the realm of the body is equally true in the sphere of the soul. There is a moral order in the world, however dimly it is discerned. No man can continue to do wrong with impunity. There is a judgement ceaselessly dogging his footsteps as he proceeds on his evil way.' The warning has been given: refusal to heed the Divine admonition can only invoke the threatened consequences, as happened in Israel's history.

The punishment of the earlier generation had been decreed, but opportunity had been afforded for repentance, and Zechariah picturesquely portrayed this in the closing verse of his brief sermon. If a man accidentally killed another, he could flee to one of the cities of refuge and there find protection from the avenger of blood, but if the latter, in hot anger, pursued and overtook the manslayer before he reached the shelter of the city, he might very well take revenge – as he was perfectly entitled to do – and wound the other mortally (Deut. 9:6). The prophet implied that judgement could have been averted by repentance, but since that generation had remained impenitent, the words and decrees (cf. Ps. 2:7; Zeph. 2:2) of God had pursued them like the avenger of blood and had overtaken them. The same word is used in a similar setting in Deut. 28:15, 45. Escape for the unrepentant was impossible. As Horace has said, 'Rarely has punishment with limping tread parted with the forerunning miscreant'. God's punitive hand had fallen upon His people and they had suffered the penalty of the seventy years of captivity. They had been forced to acknowledge that what the prophets had foretold had come to pass; what Jehovah had threatened to do He had actually done. They had evidently admitted that what had happened was a just recompense for their character and conduct. There is possibly an implication in verse 6 that the earlier generation did, in fact, turn in repentance, not only to acknowledge the justice of the punishment which they suffered (cf. Lam. 1:18), but also contritely to change their attitude to

God. The word *shub*, translated 'turn or 'return', rather implies a change of heart or behaviour.

'Turn (or return) to Me,' was the essence of the Divine plea, 'that I may turn (or return) to you.' The One, who was entitled to command, presented Himself in the guise of a suppliant, pleading with His people for a change of attitude to Him. Wm. Kelly says in his *Lectures Introductory to the Minor Prophets* (p. 432), 'Every accomplishment of His chastening on Israel ought to be a call to their souls to hear the word of Jehovah now.' He waited to turn in blessing to them if only they would turn to Him. In our own day, He still waits for the repentance and confession of His people. The slightest indication of genuine contrition for the unspiritual and carnal course we follow, the smallest sign of penitence for our waywardness and sinful desires, would at once meet with a response from a Father Who loves His children. 'Turn to Me that I may turn to you.' Untold blessing is still available; all the riches of heaven's stores are still to be appropriated if we will only turn to Him. Obsession with the material and worldly can only divert the soul from Christ and rob the Christian of the enjoyment of all He proffers. The cry is still relevant, 'Turn to Me.' The Divine plea has long remained unheeded by Israel, but today there are some small signs of an inclination towards God, and it may well be that the events of recent years are heaven's reply to these indications of penitence and contrition. It could be so for the Christian also.

CHAPTER 3

The Myrtle Grove

On the twenty-fourth day of the month Shebat (the Assyrio – Babylonian name of the eleventh month, cf. I.Macc. 16:14), three months after Zechariah's introductory message, he was given eight visions, apparently all in the course of one night. It is evident that these were not dreams, since he seems to have been in a fully conscious condition and to have been capable of holding converse with an angel, who acted as an interpreter of the visions.

The people had responded to the exhortations of Haggai and for five months had resumed with zeal and vigour the work of rebuilding the temple. Zechariah's visions were timely since they constituted an answer to some of the questions that were perplexing the Jews, but their message was very much more than that and looked beyond the present into the eschatological future. As Unger (op. cit., p. 25) says, the visions 'bridge the centuries and extend to the period of the restoration of the kingdom to Israel (Acts 1:6). They realize the ultimate in Jewish hopes and Jewish eschatology. Although all of them had an immediate and significant ministry of consolation and encouragement to the poor and feeble remnant of that day lately returned from the Babylonian exile, and desperately struggling to establish themselves in a ruined city under the heel of a foreign power, yet in no case, nor in any sense, can any of these eight visions be said to be fulfilled in the prophet's day.' Their complete fulfilment obviously lay in the future – and, to a great extent, still does.

The account of the first vision was as follows:

'On the twenty-fourth day of the eleventh month, which is the month Shebat, in the second year of Darius, the word of Jehovah came to the prophet Zechariah, the son of Berechiah, the son of Iddo, saying, I saw in the night, and behold, a man riding upon a red horse, and he stood among the myrtle trees that were in the glen: and behind him were red, sorrel and white horses. Then I said, O my Lord, what are these? And the angel who talked with me said to me, I will show you what these are. And the man who was standing among the myrtle trees answered and said, These are they whom Jehovah has sent to walk to and fro through the earth. And they answered the angel of Jehovah who was standing among the myrtle trees, and said, We have walked to and fro through the earth, and behold, all the earth sits still and is at rest. Then the angel of Jehovah answered and said, O Jehovah of hosts, how long wilt thou not have mercy on Jerusalem and the cities of Judah, against which thou hast had indignation these seventy years? And Jehovah answered with good words and comforting words the angel who talked with me. So the angel who talked with me said to me, Cry out, saying, Thus says Jehovah of hosts, Jealous am I for Jerusalem and for Zion with a great jealousy. And I am very sore displeased with the nations that are at ease: for I was but a little displeased, but they aggravated the affliction. Therefore, thus says Jehovah, I have returned to Jerusalem with compassion; my house shall be built in it, says Jehovah of hosts, and the measuring line shall be stretched out over Jerusalem. Cry yet again, saying, Thus says Jehovah of hosts, My cities shall again overflow with prosperity, and Jehovah will again comfort Zion and will again choose Jerusalem' (1:7–17).

The seventy years of captivity to Babylon, predicted by Jeremiah (Jer. 25:11, 12; 29:10) were now reaching their end and the Jews not unnaturally anticipated the early restoration of their nation, since the prophet had foretold, not only that the Chaldeans would suffer for their iniquity, but that when the period was complete, God would cause His people to return to the place from whence He had driven them. Moreover, four months earlier, Haggai had declared that there would be an universal upheaval and that all nations would be shaken (Hag. 2:6, 7), but there seemed no indication that the fulfilment of this prediction was imminent. It was partly in response to the people's perplexity that Zechariah received his first vision.

In a shady, myrtle-covered glen, he saw a troop of horsemen, led by a rider on a chestnut-coloured horse, who was subsequently described as 'the angel of Jehovah' (v. 11). The angel of Jehovah was frequently mentioned in the Old Testament, and was evidently identifiable with the Second Person of the Holy Trinity prior to His incarnation. God identified this One with Himself (Gen. 16:7–11; Exod. 3:14; 23:20 ff.; Judg. 6:12; Isa.

42:8), and described Him as the angel of His presence (Isa. 63:9, literally 'of His face'). Hagar, Abraham and Jacob all described Him as God (Gen. 16:13; 22:11, 14; 48:15, 16), and He accepted sacrifices offered to God (Judg. 6:17–24; 13:3–23). Yet the angel of Jehovah was clearly depicted in the Old Testament as the messenger of God and it was in that capacity that He appeared in Zechariah's vision. (Others are termed 'sons of God' and 'angels' in the Scriptures, but the One who alone is the revealer of God, cf. John 1:18, is *par excellence the* Son and *the* Angel of Jehovah.)

The prophet referred to other horses, but patently these also bore riders. Their leader was described as an angel and these other horsemen were obviously angels or messengers of God too. These angelic horsemen rode chestnut, sorrel and white horses, and some expositors have attempted to identify the colours with particular judgements (war, famine, disease, conquest, etc.), but it is a little difficult to sustain this interpretation. It is by no means certain whether a specific colour or colours were implied by the term 'sorrel' (or 'bay' or 'speckled'), and this may have been left vague in order not to distract attention from the primary purpose of the vision.

To enable the prophet to understand the vision and its meaning, an angel stood by his side to answer his questions and to enlighten him regarding the significance of what had been said. The Divine message was normally imparted direct to the Old Testament prophets and not through an intermediary. This unusual feature of an interpreting angel is also found, however, in Daniel (Dan. 7:16; 8:16; 9. 21 ff.) and in Revelation (Rev. 17:1 ff; 21:9 ff.). The interpreting angel was not, of course, identical with the angel of Jehovah.

The myrtle was 'a beautiful shrub, with glossy, dark green leaves and white starlike clusters of fragrant flowers, whose leaves exhaled their richest odour only when bruised'. It is indigenous to Palestine and formerly grew in rich profusion there. Its fragrant blossom was worn by brides; and its dark berries were edible. Hadassah (myrtle) was a popular name for girls and was borne, of course, by Esther. Myrtle branches were among those used in the construction of the booths in which the people lived for a week at the harvest time at the feast of tabernacles (Neh. 8:15). The tree was regarded as the symbol of joy and happiness, and Isaiah declared that, in the future days of blessing, the thorn and brier would give place to the fir and myrtle (Isa. 55:13). Many commentators regard the myrtle as symbolic of Israel, and the shady myrtle grove of the vision as a picture of the nation's state of humiliation at that time. The Jewish Yalkut, for example, says that the angel 'was standing among the myrtles which were in the *metzullah* (depths). Now myrtles (*hadassim*) mean nothing else than saints, as it is said (Esther 2:7), and he was bringing up Hadassah (Esther), and the depths mean nothing else than Babylon.' But this can hardly be regarded as a satisfactory interpretation of the vision. The fact that the angel of Jehovah took his stance in the dark valley has been regarded as an indication of our Lord's deliberate association of Himself with His people in their troubled and down-trodden condition. Although this is not the primary significance of the vision, it is, nevertheless, true that the Lord has always made His presence felt (and still does) when His people are called upon to walk through the dark valleys of life. He never leaves them to walk alone in their troubles and tribulations. Indeed, it is in the dark hour of trial that we prove the reality of His presence. Many can echo the words of the psalmist, 'though I walk through the valley of the shadow of death, I will fear no evil: for Thou art with me' (Ps. 23:4).

Darius had organized couriers and posts throughout the Persian empire and his military bands and reconnoitring patrols continually traversed the countries, not only to maintain peace and order, but also to keep the court fully acquainted with the conditions in every part of the empire from the Hellespont to the Indus. The vision made clear that the Supreme Ruler of the universe was no less active. In reply to the prophet's inquiry, he was informed by the captain of the troop (the angel of Jehovah) that the horsemen had been sent forth by God to traverse the whole earth – evidently for the purpose of ascertaining the conditions prevailing, for they subsequently returned to their leader with reports of what they had found. Although God is both omniscient and omnipresent, it would seem that He employs His servants to report upon conditions throughout His dominions. (See also Job. 1 and 2, where it was disclosed that He required – and presumably still does periodically – an account of the stewardship of mighty spirit beings.) Having surveyed the whole of the world, the reconnaissance troop returned to report that the universal picture was one of quiet tranquillity. Historically this was true at the date of the vision – the second year of Darius' reign. To quote Barnes (op. cit., p. 24), 'The Persian King, after crushing Gaumata or Bardiya (Pseudo-Smerdis) in Media, passed the Tigris, defeated Nidintu-Bel, the claimant to the Babylonian throne, in two battles, and captured Babylon. . . . After this capture of the capital of western Asia, Zechariah might well say, "All the earth sitteth still and is at rest," for though Darius speaks in the Behistun Inscription of a series of revolts which followed, yet most of these occurred in lands remote from Judah, and great Babylon itself remained for a long time in the firm grasp of Darius. As we see from Ezra 6:1, 2, communication between Judah and Babylon and Ecbatana was maintained, and this could hardly have been the case, if the confusions of the Persian empire at this period were as great as they are sometimes said to have been.'

'All the world sits still and is at rest,' was the unanimous report of the angelic members of the troop. There was no sign of the predicted upheaval which was to result in Judah's blessing (Hag. 2:6, 7). It was this fact that was disturbing the returned exiles and causing them to ask when God intended to fulfil His word, and this first vision was given in order to bring their queries to the surface and to provide an answer to them. Identifying Himself with His people, the angel of Jehovah referred to the seventy years during which God had been vehemently and justifiably angry against the nation of Judah, and asked how long His mercy was to be withdrawn from Jerusalem and the cities of Judah. (Laetsch suggests that the seventy years may not refer to the period of the exile, 605–536 B.C. see, Dan. 1:1 ff., but to that from the destruction of Jerusalem and the depopulation and devastation of the country, i.e. from 586 B.C., see 2 Chron. 36:17–21, but it seems more appropriate to relate it to the exile: that had been the specific punishment for the nation's sins). In 520 B.C. the appointed period of judgement had expired: was the Divine indignation still to continue? The angel of Jehovah became the nation's intercessor with God, just as He is still the advocate of His people today (1 John 2:1).

Heaven's reply came in terms of comfort and sympathy (not to the angel of Jehovah, who knew the answer, but to the interpreting angel), and the interpreting angel was instructed to transmit the message to the prophet and he, in turn, was to convey it, with a loud voice of proclamation, to the people. God had used the nations as His instrument for the castigation of His people, but the nations had grossly exceeded their commission. They had cruelly maltreated the Jews, had dispossessed them of their property, and had dispersed them far and wide. At this aggravation, God's wrath against Judah for her sins had melted into pity, and He declared that He was exceedingly jealous or, perhaps, extremely zealous on behalf of Jerusalem and Zion. As another says, 'He will make His people the object of His deepest concern.' On the other hand, His anger had been aroused against the nations who were living in undisturbed peace and in the enjoyment of Judah's possessions. The clear implication was that, if Judah had suffered so grievously for her sins, her oppressors would pay dearly for all they had done to increase her burden of suffering. If the words had their significance two and a half millennia ago, how much greater force there is in them in view of the terrible experiences of Jewry over the centuries and particularly during the twentieth century. That the period of travail is not yet ended is plain from the prophetic word, but Matt. 25 makes it clear that there will be a day of reckoning, and it seems evident that God will soon rise up to take vengeance on His people's oppressors. It is a Divine principle, not only that the wicked must be punished, but that those who oppose or afflict God's people must pay the penalty for their crime (Matt. 25:31–46).

Jehovah then declared that He had returned to Jerusalem with compassion (or 'mercies'). He had promised that, if they would return to Him, He would return to them (Zech. 1:3). The intercession of the angel of Jehovah had been an indication of a change of heart on the part of the remnant who had returned to the land – real, even if scarcely perceptible – and a faithful God honoured His word. His return, as A. C. Gabelein has pointed out in his *Studies in Zechariah* (p. 20), 'does not mean a spiritual return or a return of God's mercies to Jerusalem only, but it means likewise the literal return when He appears the second time; and connected with this same appearing of the great Jehovah in Jesus Christ will be seen the shekinah cloud as Israel had it in the wilderness and their first temple. . . . The

Lord had withdrawn from His people. . . . The Lord being absent in His person from His people, Israel is forsaken, the land desolate. There can be no true restoration of Israel till He has come whose right it is.' That the words had a direct application to those to whom they were addressed at the time, there can be no question, but they clearly have an eschatological significance as well. The past historical perfect can surely be construed in this case (as in many others) as a prophetic perfect, implying with certainty that an event still future is regarded as having already taken place. The restoration of the shekinah glory and the realization of Jehovah's presence in the midst of His people may not yet have occurred but, in the Divine purposes, the programme is deemed to be already complete.

The consequences of God's turning to Judah were then detailed. First of all the temple would be rebuilt. If the Divine presence was again to be known among the chosen people in the shekinah cloud of glory, there must be a dwelling-place. The temple was already in course of construction and the work was actually completed four years later (Ezra 6:15). But the promise obviously looked beyond the immediate fulfilment in Zerubbabel's temple and anticipated the establishment of the millennial temple described by Ezekiel, into which the shekinah glory could again take up residence (Ezek. 40–42; Isa. 2:2, 3).

At an earlier date, Jerusalem had been measured for destruction (2 Kings 21:13), but it was now to be measured for the purpose of planning its rebuilding, which was accomplished seventy years later by Nehemiah (Neh. 6:15). Again, however, the prophecy obviously looked on beyond Nehemiah's day to a rebuilding of the metropolis in a future day, when God will 'create Jerusalem a rejoicing and her people a joy' (Isa. 65:18).

Furthermore, the material blessings accruing to the other cities of Judah were to be so great that prosperity would cause them to expand far beyond their prescribed boundaries. Some expositors have suggested that the meaning is that other cities owned and blessed of God would be scattered through the land, but it is more probable that the term 'My cities' refers primarily, if not entirely, to cities already existent. This third promise was partially fulfilled in the times of the Hasmonean princes of the Maccabean period, but it also patently anticipated another day in which the Holy Land will experience untold millennial blessing.

Finally God declared that He would show tenderness to Zion and would set His choice upon Jerusalem. By inference, the city would become His dwelling-place amidst His people. Here again, the complete fulfilment of the promise has not yet been experienced. As Wm. Kelly (op. cit., p. 442) remarks 'these words were uttered after the return from captivity. Consequently this return could not furnish the complete fulfilment of the divine assurance, though it was no doubt a pledge of it. Therefore the object of these words was not to make them contented with the measure of mercy already shown them, but to use the present as a ground to look for greater blessing which grace has in store. . . . As far as the return from Babylon is concerned, it was already accomplished; and there has never been a return since, but another and worse scattering. It is plain and certain, therefore, that God intimates a fresh return. 'He shall yet comfort Zion and shall yet choose Jerusalem.' The establishment of a Jewish state in 1948 and the return of so many Jews, which has taken place during the present century, may be a preparation for the day which is still to come.

Behind all the changing scenes of life, the Divine purpose remained immutable and sure. What God had pledged through Jeremiah and Haggai, He would perform. Today the wicked may seem to flourish, and the rebellious world to continue its course unchecked, but God's will must ultimately triumph, and blessing will then be the portion of His people.

CHAPTER 4

The Gentile Powers

Zechariah's first vision had concluded with a promise of blessing and prosperity, but before this could become effective, it was obviously necessary for the power of Judah's oppressors to be broken. Only a remnant of Judah had returned to the land: a large number still remained in Babylonia. A relatively small number of Israel may possibly have accompanied the exiles in their return, but the great majority of the people of the northern kingdom were still exiled in the land formerly occupied by Assyria. The fulfilment of the Divine pledge of blessing must have seemed wellnigh impossible, even if it was restricted to Judah, but even more so if it was regarded as applicable also to Israel (as might perhaps be deduced from the second vision). There were enemies without and within, there were obstacles and hindrances, and there was also the people's own sinful and guilty condition, all of which must first be dealt with. Priority was evidently to be given to the external forces which affected the people, and the second vision disclosed that every antagonistic power and nation was to be destroyed, and the way prepared for the implementation of the Divine purpose. As in the first vision, however, it seems evident that, while the prophecy clearly had its primary relevance to the time in which it was uttered and to the immediate benefit of the people of that date, its full significance extended far beyond that comparatively small remnant and stretched over the centuries to the end of the age, its complete fulfilment being patently linked with the Second Advent of Christ.

The account of the vision is brief.

'Then I lifted up my eyes and saw, and behold four horns! And I said to the angel who talked with me, What are these? And he answered me, These are the horns which have scattered Judah, Israel and Jerusalem. And Jehovah showed me four artificers. Then I said, What are these coming to do? And he spoke saying, These are the horns which scattered Judah, so that no man lifted up his head; but these are come to terrify them, to cast down the horns of the nations, who lifted up their horn against the land of Judah to scatter it' (1:18–21).

In the vision of the myrtle glen, God had declared His sore displeasure with the nations whom He had employed as instruments of punishment for His people. Their brutal treatment of Judah, which far exceeded the terms of the commission which He had given them (without, of course, their realizing the true reason for their subjugation of the people and their devastation of the land), was, by implication, to invoke Divine chastisement of themselves, but no indication was given of the specific means by which their punishment would be inflicted. The second vision supplied this information, although in barest outline, making it plain that oppression does not go unobserved and that the Almighty always reserves a commensurate retribution for the malignance of the persecutor.

Zechariah was doubtless bowed in meditation at the scene of the myrtle glen and the revelation it gave that the Supreme Ruler takes cognizance of every happening in His universe. But when he lifted up his eyes, it was to see four horns, which the angel interpreted as the powers which had scattered Judah, Israel and Jerusalem. No fuller description was given of the horns, either as regards their nature and composition, or as to whether they were attached to beasts or to some other object, or were merely floating loosely in the air. The intention was obviously to focus attention on the horns and not to divert it to any other particular feature. The introduction of animals, for example, would inevitably have resulted – as has happened with so many other details in prophecy – in speculation and argument regarding their significance or identity, and this was plainly not pertinent to the message of the vision.

A horn is a familiar Biblical symbol of honour (1 Sam. 2:1; Job 16:5) or of power – regal, political, religious or military (Pss. 75:4, 5; 92:10; Jer. 48:25; Dan. 7:24; 8:3, 4; Amos 6:13; Rev. 17:12). In this instance, the angel's explanation made it clear that the horns were figurative of the great nations or empires which had not only oppressed Israel and Judah, but had driven them out of their lands or had forcibly deported them.

It is probably useless to speculate on the identity of the powers represented by the four horns. It seems evident that they were human agencies and not angelic ministers as has sometimes been suggested. Some expositors have identified those powers with Pul, Shalmaneser, Sennacherib and Nebuchadnezzar. Others have seen in them a reference to the Persians, Alexander of Macedon, Antiochus of Syria, and Ptolemy of Egypt. Others again have suggested that the horns depicted Assyria, Chaldea, Egypt and Persia. More recent writers have queried whether it is possible to relegate the application to ancient history and to ignore the sufferings inflicted upon the Jewish race in medieval times and, in our own twentieth century, by Germany, Russia, China, etc. Some of the interpretations are clearly fallacious: the Persians and Macedonians, for example, could hardly be described strictly as enemies of the Jews, while others of the nations and leaders could not properly be said to have dispersed, or 'scattered' God's people. The powers represented by the horns are specifically stated to have been those who 'scattered Judah, Israel and Jerusalem'. The more common interpretation is that Zechariah's vision referred to the same four powers as those portrayed in Daniel's prophecy (Dan. 2 and 7). viz. Babylonia, Medo-Persia, Greece and Rome. Certainly, if the view is taken that the vision covers the whole period of 'the times of the Gentiles', i.e. from the days of Nebuchadnezzar to the return of the Lord Jesus Christ to earth, it is difficult to find a more satisfactory explanation, although it may be questioned whether the description given in the vision is completely applicable to the second and third of these world empires. The fact that only four horns are mentioned has sometimes been assumed to have reference to the four cardinal points of the compass and, therefore, to be indicative of the universality of the hostility to Israel and Judah. On the north, for instance, they were faced by the active opposition of Assyria, Chaldea and Samaria; on the south by Egypt; on the west by Philistia; and on the east by Moab and Ammon. But this seems to conflict with the clear implication that only four powers were concerned.

The horns were stated to have scattered God's people. The relentless rage of the nations was, in fact, poured out upon the Jews, and the Gentile powers tossed and gored and dispersed them as dust is driven by the wind (cf. Exod. 32:20; Isa. 30:22). Barnes says (op. cit., p. 32), 'No doubt the Chaldeans carried away thousands of the Jews into captivity in Babylonia, but the allusion here is rather to the neighbours of Judah, who forwarded the work of depopulation begun by Nebuchadnezzar (cf. verse 15). Thus the Tyrians sold many of the Jews beyond the sea (Joel 3:3–6), and the Edomites carried off captives under cover of the Chaldeans (Obad. 11). There were exiles in Syria, Egypt, and the Mediterranean lands, as well as in Chaldea (2:6).' The implication is more than a mere dispersing of the people. It is rather the thorough 'winnowing' of them as grain was winnowed, indicating a severe and intensive action. Israel was said to have suffered as well as Judah. It has been suggested that the inclusion of the name of Israel was due to a subsequent interpolation of a scribe, but there is no reason to assume that Israel was excluded in the angel's explanation. It is clear from later sections of the book that the ultimate blessing of the whole nation was envisaged. The ten tribes of Israel were not lost, so far as God was concerned: they have merely been dispersed among the heathen, and one day will be restored to their own land as predicted by many of the prophets.

'God has for every hostile power which has sinned and sins against His people a correspondingly greater power to overcome it, break it in pieces, and cast it down,' says Gaebelein (op. cit., p. 23), and this was confirmed by the remaining details of the vision. As the prophet realized the strength and power of his people's foes and their ruthless determination to drive them out of their land, he might well have been depressed. What possible hope could there be? The Jews had been captive in a land whose rulers suffered no intractability and tolerated no intransigence. Their position seemed utterly hopeless. How could God possibly fulfil His pledges? Similar doubts may arise in the minds of believers today, when they realize the tremendous weight of opposition that exists and their general inability to meet it. But God's purposes can never be frustrated.

Zechariah was accordingly shown four artificers or technicians (the word used is applicable to skilled workers in wood, metal or stone – see Exod. 35:35; Deut. 27:15; Isa. 44:12, 13; 2 Sam 5:11), who had come upon the scene to terrify or to throw into a state of panic the powers represented by the horns (cf. Jer. 7:33), and vehemently to cast them down. The instruments used by these four 'carpenters', as they are decribed in the A.V., were not mentioned, and no clue was afforded regarding the identity of the workmen who were to enfeeble the great world powers. It has sometimes been suggested that they represented the four sore judgements of Ezek. 14:21 – the sword, famine, wild beast and pestilence – or, alternatively, that the reference was to mighty spiritual forces. But as the oppressors were human, it seems more logical to conclude that the counter-active agencies were human also. Each empire which has appeared upon the world's stage has been swept away in due course and replaced by another. Those, which have been the cause of trouble and tribulation to Israel and Judah, have suffered at the hands of their successors, and the prophetic word indicates that the powers which attack God's earthly people will ultimately meet with a retributive fate at the hands of the Son of God. Isa. 2:10–22 and Rev. 6 to 16 reveal something of the horrors of the future as well as of the terror of those upon whom the Divine judgements fall.

The 'nations who lifted up their horn against the land of Judah to scatter it' were to be thrown down by the four workmen. Like ferocious beasts they had charged their victims in an attempt to gore and maim. Their assault had been so fierce and unrestrained that the Jew had not even the strength to lift up his head: their inhumanity and terrible maltreatment (and often sadistic torture) of the sufferers had destroyed the latter's hopes and eventually even the will to resist. This accords with the picture painted by history.

But retribution was inevitable. None could attack God's people with impunity. The arrogant persecutors would be terrified by the instruments of God's punitive hand. The vision does not refer only to the past: it undoubtedly anticipates a day which is still future, when all Israel's foes will suffer at the hands of Messiah for their insolent cruelty and malice, and Israel and Judah (eventually one nation again) will finally enter into blessing. 'Jews take comfort in the ancient prophecies of the Hebrew seers,' says a writer of their own race, 'but history also points to the fact that though the Jews have lived by "the bread of tears", yet from the time of the triumphant proclamation on the Egyptian stele of the Pharaoh Menremptah, in the thirteenth century B.C., recording that the rebellious Israelites in Palestine had been utterly defeated – "Israel is desolated, its seed is not" – destiny appears to have ordained that this people shall not perish from the earth.'

There must be an answer to Israel's sufferings. The pogroms of Europe, the untold savagery and bestiality, bitter hatred and consistent hostility, must meet with a reply. Referring to the conditions after the First World War, the writer just quoted describes the chauvinism that arose in the new states 'that came to be regarded as essential to the assertion of a national individuality from which the Jews, as an ethnical and religious minority, were to be excluded. . . . The liberal professions were gradually closed to the Jews by the adoption of a numerous clausus at the universities. . . . The economic boycott of Jewish traders was made more effective by the increasing nationalization of commerce and industry, and ultimately they suffered the unleashing of the unbridled fury of Nazi Germany, when it was said, "Their temples have been destroyed by dynamite or deliberately devastated, and the scrolls of the law defiled; the State has confiscated their property and deprived them of the means of livelihood; they have suddenly been driven from their homes like dumb cattle and confined to the meanest streets; they have, as pariahs, been banned from the society of their non-Jewish neighbours",' and finally their lives were taken from them. A holy and righteous God must repay their persecutors and this is what the vision implied.

The lesson is not only for the Jews. When evil is in the ascendancy and the floods of trouble burst upon God's people today, we may always rest confidently in the assurance that nothing will frustrate the Divine purpose for the believer. Opposition may mass against us in terrifying volume, but eventually the forces of darkness will be overthrown and the glory of the Eternal will shine out in delivering power. God *will* redeem His pledges.

CHAPTER 5

The Measurement of the City

In the first vision God declared His jealousy for Jerusalem and His anger at the nations which had oppressed her, and announced that He would again choose Jerusalem. The second vision anticipated the ultimate defeat of the nations in question and the consequent removal of all obstacles to Judah's blessing, and referred to words of comfort being given by Jehovah. The third vision then logically provided a picture of Jerusalem's future prosperity and blessing and, as one writer says, it was virtually 'an amplification and realistic unfolding of the "comfortable words" in the second vision.' The vision fell into two parts, the first dealing with the city (2:1–5) and the second with the nation (2:6–13). The first part was relatively brief.

'I lifted up my eyes again and looked, and behold a man with a measuring line in his hand. Then I said, Where are you going? And he said to me, To measure Jerusalem, to see what is its breadth and what is its length. And behold, the angel who talked with me went forth, and another angel went forth to meet him, and he said to him, Run, speak to the young man yonder, saying, Jerusalem shall be inhabited as towns without walls because of the multitudes of men and cattle in it. For I will be to her a wall of fire round about, says Jehovah, and will be for glory in the midst of her' (2:1–5).

In the same pattern as the first two visions, the third cannot be limited to the immediate circumstances of the prophet's own day, but evidently related to the whole of the period up to the return of Christ to the earth. As Zech. 14:2, 4 indicates, at the time of the second advent, Jerusalem will have suffered the ravages of war, its walls will have been battered, its treasures looted, and half of its people carried away. Then the Mount of Olives will split in two and the whole city will naturally be affected physically by the upheaval. It will obviously be necessary for the metropolis to be entirely rebuilt, and this was principally what the third vision envisaged.

Zechariah saw a man going forth with a measuring line and

was told, in response to his inquiry, that the man's object was to measure the length and breadth of the city – presumably to determine the ground plan and to mark the proposed location of the walls and buildings, with the evident intention of rebuilding the strong walls of a mountain fortress. As the prophet watched, the interpreting angel stepped forward, but another angel intervened with an urgent message to the interpreting angel. It is not clear whether the message was to be conveyed to Zechariah or to the man with a measuring line: it was addressed to 'this young man' or 'the young man yonder', who may very well have been the prophet himself, but the point is of little consequence, for the message was plain. The man with a measuring line was a new character in the *dramatis personae.* It is not apparent whether the angel who halted the interpreting angel was also a new character or whether he was identical with the angel of Jehovah. The term 'young man' (*naar*) was probably more appropriate to Zechariah himself. In other words, the message was for him and not for the man who was about to survey the city.

In the past Jerusalem had been measured before its destruction, as an indication that the whole city was to be brought under the judicial hand of the Almighty (2 Kings 21:13; Lam. 2:8), but in the first vision God had declared that the temple would be rebuilt and the measuring line stretched forth upon the city – obviously to measure it for the purpose of planning its reconstruction as in the third vision. There are other interesting prophecies regarding the use of the measuring line, e.g. in Ezek. 40–42 in regard to the measurement of the millennial temple and in Rev. 11 in connection with the measurement of the heavenly temple. It is not obvious whether the measurement actually proceeded in Zechariah's vision or whether the purpose of the angelic intervention was to arrest the action on the ground that it was inappropriate or virtually pointless.

It was disclosed by the intervening angel that Jerusalem was to be no more a citadel, dependent for its strength and defence upon massive walls and fortifications. Its population and material prosperity were to be so great that walls would be impracticable. An earlier prophet had already said, 'your waste and desolate places and devastated land shall even now be too narrow because of the inhabitants. . . . The children of your bereavement shall yet say in your ears, The place is too narrow for me: give me room to dwell in' (Isa. 49:19, 20). Zechariah's prophecy now declared that so great would be the influx of men and cattle into Jerusalem that the city would overflow into open villages on the mountainside and its extent would be beyond measurement. The A.V. refers to 'towns without walls' and the R.S.V. to 'villages without walls' but as David Baron points out (op. cit., p. 58), 'the word strictly describes "plains", or an open country in which there is nothing to circumscribe the inhabitants, or to prevent them from spreading themselves abroad: thus in Ezek. 38:11 it is used of the land where people dwell in peace and prosperity, "without walls, bolts or gates", in contrast to those in walled cities'. Older commentators, as an indication of its possible future extent, have quoted the particulars of the city in the time of Alexander the Great, when Jerusalem was fifty stadia in circumference and was inhabited by 120,000 men. But what is envisioned in Zechariah is something very much vaster, with people living in complete peace and freedom and expanding at will.

The prophecy referred to the multitude of cattle in the city (v. 4) and the appropriateness of this has been questioned but, as Barnes (op. cit., p. 35) points out, 'ancient cities contained space for cattle' (see Jer. 33:10, 13; Jonah 4:11), and it would appear strange to a pastoral people if no provision was made for the accommodation of flocks and herds in the area of the city.

There would be no need for walls, since Jehovah promised Himself as their defence. He would be a protective wall of fire around the city. As the caravan camping in the wilderness sets fires around the encampment to keep off marauders and wild animals, so the Almighty would become a continuous ring of fire around His people. No other defence would be required if He was their protection. Their security was assured. None could assail or overthrow that city. Although the promise was made to Judah and is yet to be fully implemented in a coming day, it is still applicable to God's people today. The one who has sheltered in Christ is absolutely safe and secure. He is surrounded by a wall of fire and no foe can touch or destroy Him.

Moreover, Jehovah declared that He would be for glory in the midst of Jerusalem. In other words, the shekinah glory, which once filled the holy of holies of the tabernacle and the temple, would return to the city – not to be restricted as formerly to a hidden shrine, but to fill the whole of the city with glory (cf. Ps. 3:3). Ezekiel foretold the return of this shekinah to the future millennial temple (Ezek. 43:1–5), but Zechariah's vision is of an even greater and fuller revelation of God. In the past there had been a mysterious cloud of light, seen dimly through the cloud of incense by the high priest once a year. But, by implication, Jehovah now promised the display of the unveiled glory of God for the constant and continual occupation of every citizen of Jerusalem. During Israel's exodus and journeyings, the angel of Jehovah associated Himself with the pillar of cloud and fire, by which the nation was guided and protected, and inferentially it will be the same One (now accepted as Messiah) who will dwell in the midst of the city in a future day. The description given is evidently of the New Jerusalem, of which the seer of the Apocalypse said centuries later, 'the city had no need of the sun, neither of the moon, to shine in it: for the glory of God did lighten it, and the Lamb is its light' (Rev. 21:23). Zechariah's description plainly anticipated the millennial age, although it has its application already to the Christian, who gazes upon the unveiled glory of God in the face of Jesus Christ (2 Cor. 4:6).

It has been said that the second part of this third vision was a lyric appended to it but having no vital relation to the first part. Sir George Adam Smith (op. cit. pp. 290, 291) maintains that it is of an earlier date than the remainder of the book. 'Israel is addressed,' he says, 'as still scattered to the four winds of heaven, and still inhabiting Babylon. While in Zechariah's own oracles and visions, Jehovah has returned to Jerusalem, His return according to this piece is still future. There is nothing about the temple; God's holy dwelling position from which He has roused Himself is heaven.' But there is good reason for the view that it refers to the exiles who remained in Babylon and that it also anticipates the future. The terms of this second part of the vision were as follows.

'Ho! ho! Flee from the land of the north, says Jehovah: for I have spread you abroad as the four winds of the heaven, says Jehovah. Deliver yourself, O Zion, that dwells with the daughter of Babylon. For thus says Jehovah of hosts, After glory has he sent me to the nations which spoiled you: for he who touches you touches the apple of his eye. For, behold, I will shake my hand over them, and they shall be a spoil to their servants: and you shall know that Jehovah of hosts has sent me. Sing and rejoice, O daughter of Zion: for lo, I come, and I will dwell in the midst of you, says Jehovah. And many nations shall join themselves to Jehovah in that day, and shall be my people: and I will dwell in the midst of you, and you shall know that Jehovah of hosts has sent me to you. And Jehovah will inherit Judah his portion in the holy land, and will again choose Jerusalem. Be silent, O all flesh, before Jehovah: for he is raised up out of his holy habitation' (2:6–13).

Over two centuries earlier, the people of Israel had been deported by the Assyrians. More than a century afterwards, the people of Judah had been carried away by the Babylonians and subsequently dispersed throughout the 127 provinces of the Persian empire from India to Ethiopia. Both Assyria and Babylonia were commonly referred to as the land of the north (Jer. 1:4; 3:18; 6:22; Zeph. 2:13) since their invasions of Israel and Judah came from that direction, and Zech. 2:7 specifically linked it with Babylon.

Jeremiah foretold that the Lord would bring His people ou of the north country and gather them from the coasts of the earth (Jer. 31:8) and from all countries whither He had driven them (Jer. 23:8). Zechariah now heard the voice of God calling upon His people to flee from the north. Barnes (op. cit., p. 35) says, 'Many captives were deposited in north Syria (Hamath, 9:2; Isa. 11:11), while others were carried further to the north-east into Assyria (Mesopotamia), (10:10; Isa. 11:11) and Media (2 Kings 17:6). . . . northern Syria remained a typical land of captivity, for thither in the first instance all these captives were taken.' Jehovah declared that He had dispersed them 'as the four winds of heaven' – a phrase which may mean either their dispersal to every part of the earth or the manner in which He had 'spread them abroad' – but now they were to flee. The immediate objects of the injunction were clearly the many exiles who had remained behind when others had returned to the land under Joshua and Zerubbabel. The injunction patently presaged the impending judgement on Babylon and was directed at securing the evacuation of the exiles before the judgement fell. Isa. 48:14, 20; Jer. 50:8, 10; 51:6, 45 specifically connect the judgement of Babylon with the escape of Judah.

Baron (op. cit., pp. 70, 71) argues that this part of the prophecy had 'only a partial reference to the times in which the prophet wrote his visions. Though a remnant had returned, by far the greater number were still in the land to which they had been exiled. Some of them had grown rich and prosperous in the strange land. Their love for Jerusalem and all that it stood for had cooled down, and they were content to become dwellers "with the daughter of Babylon". They were reluctant to leave their comfortable homes and vineyards (which they had indeed been encouraged to build and to plant, but only as temporary possessions during the seventy years of the captivity, Jer. 29) for the rough journey and hard life in the desolated land. And so they are exhorted to flee out of Babylon, not only because of the goodness of the Lord which is to be shown to His people in their own land, but because of the evil which was about to overtake the country of their sojourn, and the calamities which would come on its people, occasioned probably by the two great rebellions in Babylon, and the two captures of the city of Babylon – one by Darius in person, and the other by one of his generals – which had just taken place when the prophet wrote his visions. At the same time, this call to come out of the Babylon of that time, which met with only a very partial response, was also a foreshadowing of the future, when Jehovah shall lift up His hand again a second time to recover the remnant of His people which shall be left from Assyria and from Egypt, and from Pathros and from Cush, and from Elam, and from Shinar, and from Hamath and from the islands of the sea.' The call now made, however, was, in the first instance, to the exiles in Babylon to come out and to return to their own country.

'After glory' had God sent His agent to Judah's oppressors. There is a wide variety of interpretations of this term. It can scarcely refer, as some have suggested, to the bestowal of glory in verse 5, or to the Divine acquisition of glory or a desire to acquire additional glory. The more probable significance is that the action taken was a demonstration of God's glory or a vindication of it. To quote Baron again (op. cit., p. 73), it 'means to vindicate and to display the glory of God, first in the judgements which He is to inflict on the nations who have oppressed

Israel, and then in the exhibition of His grace in the deliverance and salvation of His own people, and also in the blessing which is to come to the Gentile nations after Israel is restored, and Mount Zion becomes not only the seat of Messiah's governmental rule over the nations, but the centre of the true worship of God on the earth'. The context tends to imply that what is in view is the Second Advent of Christ in power and glory to smite the nations with the rod of His anger and to bring salvation to His people. As another has said, God's 'glory is inseparably linked with the fortunes of His people. He cannot be glorified as long as His people are disgraced and persecuted by their enemies.' That will be ended when the Son of God returns to Olivet to execute judgement upon a guilty world. The Masoretic text marks a pause after the word 'glory', so that the text might very well read, 'After glory! He has sent me. . . .'

God declared that He had sent His agent in judgement to the nations which had oppressed His people. They had afflicted His elect, who were as dear to Him as the apple of His eye. In daring anthropomorphic picture, the prophecy declared that whoever touched God's people touched God at the most tender point. The pupil of the eye is the most sensitive part of the human body (cf. Deut. 32:10; Ps. 17:8), feeling acutely the most minute injury. The maltreatment of Judah affected the Divine feelings as a sudden jab would affect the contractile opening of the visual organ. When Saul of Tarsus was suddenly arrested by the Christ of the glory on the Damascus road, the Master's words of remonstrance for his persecution of His followers were significant. 'Why do you persecute *Me*?' (Acts 9:4), He asked Saul. Every attack today upon the Christian, who is a member of the body of Christ, is inevitably felt by the Head of the body. This has always been true. The Eternal so closely associates Himself with His people that their sorrows and sufferings are His.

In a menacing gesture, Jehovah declared that He would shake (or brandish) His hand (Isa. 11:15; 19:16) over those who had spoiled Judah and that they should themselves become a spoil to the people whom they had held in servitude (cf. Isa. 14:1, 2). The tables were to be turned. Laetsch says (op. cit., p. 420), 'When He shakes His hand, which formed the earth (Ps. 95:5 and makes the mountains smoke (Ps. 104:32), the proud masters will become servants, the presumptuous rulers, abject slaves. So will the glory of the Lord . . . become manifest and be gratefully praised by all His people, and acknowledged, with bitter resentment and horrified fear, by His enemies.' At an earlier date the prophet Isaiah had declared that their former oppressors would be possessed by Israel as slaves (Isa. 14:2). When this complete reversal of their fortunes occurred, it would be convincing evidence that Jehovah had sent His servant – a statement which is repeated in verse 11.

In anticipation of their salvation and of the blessings yet to be experienced, the people (portrayed as a young woman, the 'daughter of Zion') were called upon to burst forth in jubilant psalm, because Jehovah was coming and would dwell in their midst (cf. Isa. 12:6; Zeph. 3:14, 15). Perowne says (op. cit., pp. 77, 78) that 'this prophecy had a fulfilment, when the temple was rebuilt and the worship of God was resumed on Mount Zion. But it had a higher fulfilment when "the Word was made flesh and dwelt among us" (John 1:14; Mal. 3:1), and the promise of the Gentiles being joined to the Lord (v. 11) was also accomplished. It awaits its highest fulfilment in both particulars in the times that are yet future (Rev. 7:15; 21:3, 22–26).' The coming referred to was not merely our Lord's first advent. In view of the context and the statements immediately following it seems clear that it is the second advent that is primarily envisioned. The Almighty, in the person of the Messiah, is to break into time once more and His coming will bring joy and gladness to His people and, in all His wonder and glory, He will then actually dwell in their midst. God will again take up residence on earth, not this time in humiliation and lowliness, but in all His power and majesty.

In that day (a term which tends to confirm the millennial setting of the scene), the prophecy declared that many nations would join themselves to Jehovah. Through the preaching of the gospel of the coming King by Jewish missionaries and ultimately by the revelation of the Eternal, multitudes of Gentiles will be converted and will, of their own volition, join themselves to Him, precisely as the prophet Jeremiah had previously predicted (Jer. 50:4, 5). Even during the period of the great tribulation, it is clear that many Gentiles will be saved (Rev. 7:9, 10; 14:1–4), and when the revelation of the Messiah comes at His appearing, others will be attracted to Him (Isa. 56:3, 6). Again the promise was repeated that Jehovah would dwell in the midst of His people, and once more God's messenger declared that, by the fulfilment of what had been predicted, Judah would know that God had sent him.

The conversion of Gentiles in such large numbers might possibly give rise to doubt whether the Divine pledges to Israel had been annulled or abrogated in some way. The original election of Israel was an irrevocable one, and nothing will alter it. (See *Will there be a Millennium?* by F. A Tatford). The character and conduct of the people were irrelevant: the choice was not conditioned by their behaviour. They are the portion and inheritance of Jehovah (cf. Deut. 9:24; 32:9), His portion in the holy land (the only occurrence in Scripture of the term 'the holy land'). The apostle Paul indicates that, during the present era, 'the riches of His glorious inheritance in the saints' has reference to the church (Eph. 1:18), but in the millennial age, Israel will be Jehovah's inheritance (Isa. 19:25).

Once more the Almighty stated that He would again choose Jerusalem: in other words, He would demonstrate the immutability of His original choice. Feinberg says in *God Remembers* (p. 51), the statement 'does not imply that God must choose Israel afresh, but that now, at long last, He will be able to manifest to the world the immutable character of His original choice and its practical outworking in renewed, restored and resettled Israel.' The fact will be established beyond all possible doubt. This is God's chosen city, the place where He will set His name.

The whole scene is obviously of the commencement of the millennial period of bliss and happiness, peace and prosperity. The nations will have been dealt with, the sinner trampled under foot, and the glory of Jehovah will cover the earth as the waters cover the sea. 'Be silent, all flesh, before Jehovah,' came the imperative (cf. Hab. 2:20). The judicial glory of God was about to be manifested and all might well fear for He was coming to judge the earth. He had awakened or roused Himself up from the habitation of His holiness. All mankind might well be hushed in awe at His presence. He does not, of course, actually sleep. 'He who keeps Israel will neither slumber nor sleep' (Ps. 121:3, 4). When the earth was at rest and evil continued unchecked, it must have seemed as though God was asleep. But now there was no doubt regarding His activity. He had risen up out of the habitation of His holiness (Deut. 26:15; Jer. 25:30), and was about to issue forth to succour His people and to discomfit their foes.

CHAPTER 6

The Cleansing of the Priesthood

The preceding visions had disclosed the retribution to be meted out to the Gentile powers and the ultimate blessing of the nation of Israel. But before the people could be restored to communion with God, it was essential for their defilement to be removed, and it was with this matter that the third chapter of the book was concerned.

Seraiah, the grandfather of Joshua, the high priest, was among those taken captive by Nebuchadnezzar after the sacking of Jerusalem and he was subsequently slain by his captor at Riblah (2 Kings 25:18–21). His son, Josedech, was also among the deportees (1 Chron. 6:15) and Joshua was evidently born in Babylon. During the lifetime of Josedech, while the temple was in ruins and the people in captivity, the high priesthood had virtually been in abeyance, since the exercise of the sacerdotal functions was clearly impossible. With the return of the exiles and, Josedech having apparently died prior to that return, Joshua had become his legitimate successor as high priest. Now, after fifty-two years, the office had again been filled, and Joshua stood as the representative of his people before God, and the question arose of his suitability to fill the sacred office. The high priest, as Leupold says in his *Exposition of Zechariah* (p. 64), 'represents and practically impersonates Israel in his holy office. For the nation he prays; for it he enters the holy place; he bears the nation's guilt. We must not, therefore, refer the issues and implications of this chapter to Joshua as an individual, nor merely to Joshua, the high priest. We must conclude that *his* condition is *Israel's* condition, *his* acquittal a typical way of expressing *theirs*; the words of comfort and assurance given *him* apply with equal validity to *them*.' God referred to His choice of *Jerusalem* and not of *Joshua* (vv. 2 and 4) and verse 9 states that the iniquity of the *land* has been removed. Zechariah's next vision was thus concerned with the cleansing of the priesthood as representative of the cleansing of the people.

'And he showed me Joshua the high priest standing before the angel of Jehovah, and Satan standing at his right hand to accuse him. And Jehovah said to Satan, Jehovah rebuke you, O Satan; even Jehovah who has chosen Jerusalem rebuke you. Is not this a brand plucked out of the fire? Now Joshua was clothed with filthy garments, and was standing before the angel. And he answered and spoke to those who were standing before him, saying, Take away the filthy garments from him. And to him he said, Behold, I have caused your iniquity to pass from you, and I will clothe you with change of raiment. And I said, Let them put a clean mitre upon his head. So they put a clean mitre upon his head and clothed him with garments. And the angel of Jehovah was standing by. And the angel of Jehovah solemnly affirmed to Joshua, saying, Thus says Jehovah of hosts, If you will walk in my ways, and if you will keep my charge, then shall you also judge my house, and you shall also keep my courts, and I will give you a place of access among these who stand by. Hear now, O Joshua, the high priest, you, and your fellows who sit before you: for they are men of portent. For behold, I will bring forth my servant, the Branch. For behold the stone, that I have laid before Joshua; upon one stone are seven eyes; behold, I will engrave the graving of it, says Jehovah of hosts, and I will remove the iniquity of this land in one day. In that day, says Jehovah of hosts, shall you invite every man his neighbour under the vine and under the fig tree' (3:1–10).

One of the most amazing features of the Christian era is that, through the work of Calvary, the believer has the right of access at all times into the immediate presence of God – the *sanctum sanctorum* of the celestial heights (Heb. 10:19). Under the Mosaic economy, by contrast, the individual's approach to God was solely through the medium of the priesthood, and even the high priest could enter the Divine presence only once a year (Lev. 16:2, 29–34). Since the priesthood thus represented the nation, it was essential that no taint of sin or defilement should attach to those who officiated in the temple service, and it was, therefore, required that the priest should offer first for his own sins before he made any sacrifices on behalf of the people (Heb. 7:27). Zechariah must consequently have been gravely disturbed at the vision to which his attention was drawn by the interpreting angel, for the high priest stood in the presence of God attired in filthy robes.

Joshua was standing before the angel of Jehovah and it has been suggested that the term employed was that commonly used of an assembly at the royal court, when nobles and officials stood in attendance upon their sovereign, to learn his will and to carry out his behests. But the expression, 'to stand before Jehovah', was consistently used in the Old Testament in a technical sense to denote the ordinary service of the priests in the sanctuary (Deut. 10:8; 2 Chron. 29:11; Judg. 20:28; Ps. 134:1; Ezek. 44:15). The implication was clearly that Joshua stood in the Divine presence in his official capacity to intercede on behalf of his people.

The description of the high priest's garments in verse 1 is amplified in verse 3, where it is specifically stated that Joshua was standing, clothed in filthy garments. The presumption that, in the description given, there is an allusion to the Roman practice of compelling an accused person to wear sordid attire unless and until his fate was determined, is obviously fallacious since the high priest was not arraigned for trial. It is clear also that there is no ground for the fantastic idea that 'an accusation had been lodged against Joshua in the Persian court', says Stanley (*Jewish Church*, vol. III, p. 103) and that 'the splendid attire of the high priest, studded with jewels, had been detained at Babylon or, at least, could not be worn without the special permission of the king; and until the accusation had been cleared away, this became still more impossible'. The clothes worn by Joshua were covered with excrement or vomit (Jer. 28:8) and were evil-smelling as well as filthy. The clothes (symbolizing the uncleanness of the priesthood and the people) were similar to those which would be worn by a foul criminal and, *prima facie*, were the irrefutable evidence that he was disqualified for his high office. How could a holy God countenance such an unclean person? The garments worn by Joshua disclosed his uncleanness. As habits or clothes are to the body, so are actions to the real man. What was visualised, of course, was not merely the defilement of the high priest, but that of the nation as a whole – their constant sins, their apostasy and their infidelity.

Also standing before the angel of Jehovah was the adversary to accuse the people's representative. In a paronomasia the inspired writer declares that Satan was there to *satanize* him –

the accuser, to accuse. The reference was clearly to a person. 'It is a favourite notion,' says Chambers (op. cit., p. 39) 'that Zechariah imported his conception of Satan from the Zoroastrian doctrine of Ahriman, the original source of all moral and physical evil, the chief of malignant spirits, the king of darkness and of death, and consequently the eternal enemy of Ormuzd, and of his kingdom of light,' but long before the Babylonian captivity, the Scriptures had clearly indicated the existence of a mighty spirit being, bitterly opposed to the Almighty. (See *The Prince of Darkness*, by F. A. Tatford).

Satan was ready to challenge Joshua's title to represent his people because of his defilement (and, by implication, his sinnership). Before the adversary could utter a word, however, the angel of Jehovah intervened and rebuked him for his presumption. The God, who had in sovereignty chosen Jerusalem, was under no compulsion to explain His ways or defend his actions (Exod. 33:19). He had brought His people out of captivity, snatching them out of the furnace of Babylon. Was it likely that He would cast back into the fire a brand which He had so recently snatched therefrom and surrender His servant (i.e. the nation and not merely Joshua) to destruction? The words probably have a prophetic significance as well as an immediate application, and the fire may refer to Israel's sufferings, in the future as well as in the past. The devil is still the accuser of God's people (Rev. 12:10), and the Christian who commits sin is particularly susceptible to his attack and is open to his accusation (1 Cor. 5:5; 1 John 5:10). What an assurance there is in the knowledge that, whatever our failure and wrongdoing, the One who died to redeem us will never allow His people to come into condemnation (John 5:24). The evil one may attack and may seek to accuse us in the presence of God, but the blood of Christ shelters us from all his assaults.

Joshua uttered no word in his own defence, and some have suggested that this was the palpable evidence of his guilt. But the Almighty had intervened before the accuser could speak and had silenced the devil before any case could be submitted. Twice the presentation of the accusation was forestalled, and there was neither opportunity nor reason for any plea to be made by the accused. His defilement was obvious, but Jehovah declared that He had caused his iniquity to pass away. His disqualification was to be removed and he was to be rendered fit to undertake his sacerdotal ministry again.

The filthy garments with which he was clad made him unfit to stand in the Divine presence, but his absolution was confirmed when the angel of Jehovah instructed the angels who stood in attendance upon him to remove the vomit-covered and excrement-bespattered clothes from Joshua. The defiled clothing was replaced by festal robes – a reference to the high priest's garments of glory and beauty (Exod. 29:4, 5; Lev. 8:7–9) thereby confirming that he was to be retained in office. As another says, 'the God of absolute holiness, justice and righteousness is, at the same time, the God of unalterable and everlasting grace, forgiving iniquity, trespasses and sin, without relinquishing the least iota of His holiness'. There may be a subtle reference in the priest's defiled clothing to the earlier description of the people as unclean and their good deeds as filthy rags (Isa. 64:6). The purification of the nation's representative may also prefigure the cleansing of the nation described in a later part of the prophecy. Whatever other message was conveyed, it was clear that none can stand in the Divine presence in his own merit: his title is dependent upon the grace of God and virtually lies in the merits of Another.

At Zechariah's cry, the mitre of the high priest (a turban of byssus or white linen) was then placed upon Joshua's head. To the mitre, of course, would be attached the golden plate with its inscription, 'Holy to Jehovah' (Exod. 28:36). Grace had adorned the high priest with clothes suitable for his ministry and functions and he now received the Divine commission to minister before God on behalf of his nation. It was always the purpose of God that Israel should act as priests on behalf of the nations of the world, but in general the people ignored the spiritual needs of others and attempted to focus the Divine blessings solely upon themselves. They failed the purpose of God. But in a future day, the nation will be universally known as 'priests of Jehovah' and 'ministers of our God' (Isa. 61:6), and the original purpose will be completely achieved.

The angel of Jehovah then solemnly affirmed to Joshua that, if he walked in God's ways and kept His ordinances, the responsibility for the administration and direction of all temple affairs would be vested in him. Furthermore he would preserve the temple courts from defilement. The inestimable privilege would also be bestowed upon him of free entry among the angels who stood in the presence of God, i.e. admission to the immediate presence of God. Unimpeded ingress would be allowed to him. So far as Israel and her representative are concerned, the complete fulfilment of the prophecy plainly relates to a period still future. The access promised to the earthly people of God is, however, already the privilege and experience of the heavenly people of today and they do not await a future day for the appropriation of this blessing.

The vision so far had been concerned with the high priest, but in verse 8 the remainder of the priests were called upon to listen to the angel of Jehovah. They were described as those who sat before Joshua – not, of course, at that particular moment, but in their official capacity. David Baron (op. cit., p. 106) says that they were 'the ordinary priests who, in meetings of the order for the purpose of discussing or deciding matters connected with their office, "sat before" the high priest, who was the president of the assembly'. The angel referred to them as 'men of portent' or 'men of sign' (the A.V. renders 'men wondered at'). C. H. H. Wright remarks, 'The vision had pictured to the eye of the priest-prophet the manner in which the priesthood of Israel, represented by Joshua, though defiled with iniquity, had been cleansed by Divine grace, and rendered acceptable to God. By that grace, priest and people had been snatched like half-burnt brands from the fire of a well-deserved punishment. That deliverance was, however, typical of a greater salvation, which the angel was now about to reveal. Hence Joshua and his fellows were typical men.' They were also symbolic of another priesthood (the New Testament holy and royal priesthood of which every true Christian is a member). They were servants of Jehovah in the temple and typical of another Servant, whom God was about to bring forth in the guise of a Branch or Sprout.

The title 'the Servant of Jehovah' was used of the nation of Israel in Jer. 30:10; 46:27 and possibly in Ezek. 28:25; 37:25 (although the Ezekiel passages may refer to Jacob personally). It is developed more fully in the prophecy of Isaiah (see e.g. Isa. 41:8; 42:19, 43:10; 44:1, 21; 45:4; 48:20) and particularly in what are usually described as the 'Servant songs', i.e.

Isa. 42:1–6; 49:1–6; 50:4–9; 52:13 to 53:12. There is a considerable difference of opinion regarding the interpretation of these passages and the Servant is variously identified as (*a*) the nation of Israel, (*b*) spiritual Israel, (*c*) ideal Israel, (*d*) a historical person (probably a religious teacher) and (*e*) an ideal individual whose appearance was still future (i.e. the Messiah). Whilst there are arguments for the theory that the references must be to a collective body, it is more logical to treat them as having a personal application. J. Skinner, in *The Book of the Prophet Isaiah* (volume II, p. xxxiii) says, 'The Servant is one who endures persecution and opposition from his own countrymen (Isa. 50:6–9) and dies the death of a martyr at their hands (53:1–9). His sufferings and death constitute an atonement for the sins of his people, so that with his stripes they are healed (53:4–6, 8). He is one also who is in conscious and perfect sympathy with Jehovah's purpose in raising him up; he is neither blind nor deaf, but alert and sensitive and responsive to the divine voice (50:4, 5).' Many of the expressions, which are used in Isaiah can scarcely apply to any other than our Lord Jesus Christ and Zech. 3:8 seems a clear prediction of the Messiah. In *The Suffering Servant in Deutero – Isaiah*, C. R. North maintains that the Servant is a soteriological messianic figure and this conclusion is really inescapable.

The second expression used by God was the Branch or Sprout. Here again, there can be little doubt that the reference was to the Messiah, of whom the title is frequently used in the Old Testament. It is significant that He was not described as a tall, stately tree, but as a shoot from the roots. With the removal of Israel and Judah from their own land, the royal house of David gradually sank into obscurity, and Calvin aptly remarks that 'so much was the dignity of that family diminished that it seemed to be a rustic, ignoble family rather than a royal one.' In such a reduced condition, the prospect of a fulfilment of the Davidic covenant of 2 Sam. 7 seemed very remote. When the royal tree was thus cut down to the ground, however, a shoot (the Messiah) sprouted out from its roots (Isa. 11:1; Job. 14:7–9), presenting a picture, as Luther says, 'of the whole of theology and the works of God; that Christ did not come till the trunk had died and was altogether in a hopeless condition'. This Branch is later described as Jehovah's servant and is represented as a mighty ruler. So closely is the name associated with the Messiah that Zechariah later spoke of Him as 'the Man whose name is the Branch' (Zech. 6:12). It is interesting to note, on the other hand, that the same One is described in Rev. 5:5 and 22:16 as 'the root of David'.

In the prophecies concerning the Branch, two Hebrew words are used. The first of these, *netser*, which means 'a shoot', is used only four times in the Old Testament (Isa. 11:1; 14:19; 60:21; Dan. 11:27). It is allied to the name of Nazareth, and the statement of Matt. 2:23 may possibly have a reference to the prophecies containing the word. The other word employed, *tsemach*, means 'a sprout' or 'a budding plant' (Isa. 4:2; 23:5; 33:15; Zech. 3:8; 6:12). The related verb, *tsamach*, is also used in Ps. 132:17 and Ezek. 24:21, which both appear relevant to the subject.

Of the occurrences of the word *netser*, the only one which has an undoubted Messianic connection is that in Isa. 11:1 which the R.V. renders, 'There shall come forth a shoot out of the stock of Jesse, and a branch out of his roots shall bear fruit.' In Isa. 10 the prophet likens the Assyrian to the mighty forests of Lebanon being hewn down under the hand of God in final destruction for, as Kay points out, 'when a cedar is cut down, it sends out no fresh suckers. Therefore, when Asshur fell, it perished.' Long before this the house of David had undergone judgement, and in Isa. 11 it is described as a stump of a tree. Out of this stump, however, there was to come forth a shoot which, although insignificant and unassuming at first, would develop into a glorious tree. As Hengstenberg writes, 'a shoot proceeding from his roots (i.e. the cut-off stem of Jesse) shall grow up into a stately fruitful tree. As a tree cut down throws out from its roots a young shoot which, at first, inconsiderable, grows up into a stately fruitbearing tree, so from the family buried in contempt and lowliness, a King shall arise who, at first humble and unheeded, shall afterwards attain to great glory.' In this prophecy there is an unmistakable picture of the two advents of the Lord Jesus Christ. Born in Bethlehem's manger, living in the comparative obscurity of despised Nazareth, in the bosom of a humble family, our Lord – to human eyes – was insignificant and unimportant. Indeed, Isa. 53:2 states that He grew up 'as a tender plant and as a root out of a dry ground', giving offence as Michaelis says, in 'that He does not rise or stand out like the cedar, but He grows up gradually'. He 'sprang from a decayed family', says Lange. 'The Davidic trunk had fallen and this was a mere sucker growing out of one of the upturned roots.' In a coming day, however, He will be accorded the place of glory and exaltation.

The many references in which the word *tsemach* is used indicate that the Branch will have not only a human but also a divine nature, for Isa. 4:2 describes Him as 'the Branch (or Sprout) of Jehovah' and 'the fruit of the land'. Hengstenberg aptly writes, 'As the words "Sprout of the Lord" denote the heavenly origin of the Redeemer, so do the words "fruit of the land" the earthly one, the soil from which the Lord causes the Saviour to sprout up.' The phrase, 'fruit of the land', has undoubtedly a reference to Num. 13:26 and Deut. 1:25, the only two other passages in which the phrase occurs, the natural fruit being regarded as a type of Christ Himself.

In Jer. 23:5 and 33:15 (300 years before Christ this was recognized by the Jews as referring to Messiah) God specifically promised to fulfil the Davidic covenant by the raising up to David of a righteous Branch (see also Ps. 132:17), who would introduce millennial blessings and sit as king and priest upon the throne of David (Zech. 3:8; 6:12). The One who commenced as a tiny shoot will eventually become a flourishing tree and the source of blessing to the whole earth.

After the reference to God's Servant, the Branch, the attention of the priests was directed to a mysterious stone, which Jehovah had laid before Joshua. Chambers sees the stone as a symbol of the covenant people, but this can hardly be regarded as tenable. It could scarely have been the foundation stone of the temple, which had been laid years before, although Baron evidently concludes that it was, for he says (op. cit., p. 117), 'According to the Talmud, the *Eben Shetiyah* – the foundation stone of the second temple, which was some inches higher than the level of the holy of holies – had the sacred Tetragrammaton (the four Hebrew letters making up the ineffable name, "Jehovah") graven upon it.' It seems more likely that the reference was rather to the headstone (cf. Zech. 4:7, 9), which would be the final stone to complete the temple. The stone is frequently used as a type of Messiah and He is often described as the chief corner stone (Ps. 118:22; Matt. 21:42; Eph. 2:20) and Daniel featured His kingdom as a stone which would crush the Gentile colossus (Dan. 2:45).

Seven eyes were directed upon the stone and it was beautified by engravings. Some have thought that the eyes were actually engraved upon the stone, but this does not seem implicit in the description given. The seven eyes seem rather to be indicative of the perfect intelligence and omniscience of the Almighty. His infinite watchfulness and care were to be fixed upon the stone, not only to make certain that no harm came to it, but also to ensure that His purpose concerning it was effected. The seven eyes are stated in Zech. 4:10 to be the eyes of Jehovah, and it is pertinent that the Lamb in Rev. 5:6 also had seven eyes. Ewald considers that 'the conception of the seven eyes of Jehovah was derived from the Persian notion of the seven Amahaspands, who surround the throne of the Supreme Being', while Barnes (op. cit., p. xxiv) maintains that Zechariah was 'explicitly claiming for the one true God the sevenfold power ascribed by the Babylonians to the Pleiades (cf. Job. 38:31) and also to the "planets" as known to them (i.e. the sun, the moon, Mercury, Venus, Mars, Jupiter and Saturn)'.

The interest of God in the stone was also indicated by the fact that He personally undertook the engraving of the stone. On the assumption that the seven eyes were not engraved on the stone, no information is given as to what was, in fact, engraved upon it.

In one day, God declared that the iniquity of the land would be removed. Under the Levitical economy, the transgressions of the nation of Israel were brought under review each year on the day of atonement and were figuratively borne away by the scapegoat into the wilderness (Lev. 16). What was envisioned in the Divine promise, however, was not the ceremonial of the annual day of atonement, but presumably the complete cleansing from defilement predicted in Zech. 13:1. The fountain to be opened for sin and uncleanness would remove all the people's guilt. The term used in verse 10 ('in that day') has an eschatological significance in Zechariah and anticipates the Second Advent of Christ to establish His kingdom upon earth.

In that day the picture would be completely transformed, and the land would enjoy peace, joy and prosperity. Neighbours would engage in social intercourse under the vine and fig tree, and gladness would prevail on every side. The conditions described have never been seen in history and it is evident that the prophecy anticipates the bliss and happiness of the millennial age. Mic. 4:4, in fact, does invest the vine and the fig tree with a millennial significance. The joy described by Zechariah follows upon the cleansing of the land and C. H. H. Wright in his *Bampton Lectures* (pp. 77, 78) pertinently points out that 'when, on the great Day of Atonement, the high priest had performed the various duties of that solemn day, he was escorted home in a festive manner, and was accustomed to give a festal entertainment to his friends. The maidens and youths of the people went forth to the gardens and vineyards with songs and dances; social entertainments took place on all sides, and universal gladness closed the festival of that solemn day.' His remarks are obviously based on the Talmud, Yoma 7:4, which is also quoted by David Baron – op. cit., p. 122. If that was true after the temporary work of that earlier age, how great will be the joy when God removes His people's defilement and reconciles them to Himself.

CHAPTER 7

The Golden Lampstand

Zechariah had seen four visions and the strain of observation and of seeking to understand the explanations provided had evidently exhausted him, so that he almost appeared to be asleep. But the revelations of the night had not yet ended, and the interpreting angel aroused him to full consciousness again. It had been disclosed that the Gentile oppressors of God's people were to be punished, that restoration of the nation to blessing was to be effected, that a cleansed priesthood was to ensure the renewal of communion with God, and that the Messiah was yet to come. The prophet may well have questioned how all this was to be accomplished, and the next vision made it clear that human ability and effort were insufficient and that Divine power alone could achieve the fulfilment of God's purpose. The lesson was again cast in illustrative form.

'Then the angel who talked with me returned and aroused me as a man aroused out of his sleep, and said to me, What do you see? And I said, I have seen and behold a lampstand all of gold, with its bowl upon the top of it, and its seven lamps on it, and seven pipes to each of the seven lamps which are on its top: and two olive trees by it, one on the right side of the bowl and the other on the left of it. So I answered and spoke to the angel who talked to me saying, What are these, my lord? Then the angel who talked with me answered and said to me, Do you not know what these are? And I said, No, my lord. Then he answered and spoke to me, saying, This is the word of Jehovah to Zerubbabel, saying, Not by might nor by power, but by my Spirit, says Jehovah of hosts. Who are you, O great mountain before Zerubbabel? Be a plain! And he shall bring forth the head-stone with shoutings, Grace, grace to it. Moreover the word of Jehovah came to me saying, The hands of Zerubbabel have laid the foundation of the house; his hands shall also complete it: and you shall know that Jehovah of hosts has sent me to you. For who has despised the day of small things? For they shall rejoice, and shall see the plummet in the hand of Zerubbabel, even these seven; they are the eyes of Jehovah, which run to and fro through the whole earth. Then answered I and said to him, What are these two olive trees on the right of the lampstand and on its left? And I answered again and said to him, What are these two olive branches which through the two golden pipes empty the golden oil out of themselves? And he answered me and said, Do you not know what these are? And I said, No, my lord. Then said he, These are the two anointed ones, who stand by the Lord of the whole earth' (4:1–14).

On the left of the altar of incense in the tabernacle stood a golden candelabrum or lampstand, which was beaten out of a talent of pure gold. It consisted of a main shaft, out of which proceeded seven branches, one upright and three on either side. On the extremities of these branches were placed seven lamps containing pure olive oil. The branches were ornamented with almond-shaped bowls, knops, and flowers, bowl or calyx, knop and flower alternately. The golden lampstand furnished the only light in the holy place and was kept burning continually. Adolph Saphir regards the vessel as an expressive symbol of our Lord Jesus Christ. 'Here', he says, 'we behold Jesus Christ, the Son of God incarnate, the light of the world; the Lord, upon whom was the Spirit of the Lord, anointing Him, to declare salvation unto the broken-hearted; the Messiah, Who came in the sevenfold plenitude of the Holy Ghost, and Who was continually revealing the Father. . . . It is as Immanuel that He is the candlestick. He came to be a mediator, to reveal God, and to bring the light of God in our hearts. He is the light of the world in such a way that sinful men, becoming one with Him, are also the light of the world. He is able to say unto His disciples, "Let your light so shine before men!"' Another writer also suggests that the lampstand symbolized the glory and the work of Christ. 'The pure gold reflects His divinity, the beaten work His sufferings, the olive oil the indwelling Holy Spirit.' In Solomon's temple, the place of the golden lampstand of the tabernacle was taken by ten golden lampstands, five standing on each side of the holy place (1 Kings 7:49). Their construction was similar to that of the one in the tabernacle, and seventy lamps, therefore, provided light for the holy place of the temple. The writer previously quoted suggests that 'the oil used for the lighting can refer only to the Holy Spirit, and the lampstands suggest the realized presence and power of the Holy Spirit in testimony'.

In Zerubbabel's temple, there was only one lampstand (1 Macc. 1:23; 4:49; see also the sculpture on the Arch of Titus), and significantly the prophet, when aroused, saw a single golden lampstand, but one which was entirely different in construction from that used in the tabernacle and the temple. The vessel he saw in vision had seven lamps and these were provided with oil from a receptacle on the top of the lampstand, this bowl or receptacle being replenished with oil from two olive trees, which stood on either side.

The purpose of the lampstands in the tabernacle and the temple was, of course, to shed light in the darkness, but the light was dependent upon the maintenance of the supply of oil for the lamps. Without the oil there could be no light. Olive oil is frequently used in the Old Testament as a type of the Holy Spirit, and it could be said of the Christian today, as much as for Israel or Judah in their day, that there can be no light or inspired witness to God, except by the power of the Holy Spirit. The greater the measure of the Spirit personally realized and experienced, the brighter will be the light of testimony. It had always been God's intention that Israel should be a light to the nations, and the lampstand in the tabernacle and those later in the temple were the constant reminder of her vocation. She failed, but the Divine purpose remains unaltered and one day she will become a light to the Gentiles (Isa. 49:6; 60:3). During His earthly life, our Lord was personally the light of the world (John 8:12; 1:9). Now, His followers are those from whom the light shines (Matt. 5:14). but they also may fail and our Lord warned the church of Ephesus of the possibility of the removal of her lampstand (Rev. 2:5) as an indication of His possible rejection of her testimony.

Zechariah's lampstand, as already indicated, was entirely different from those of the tabernacle and the temple. The lamps of those vessels were daily trimmed and supplied with fresh oil (Exod. 27:20, 21), but there was no need for this in the case of the one seen by the prophet. It had a container above it, from which the oil flowed by gravity to the seven lamps by forty-nine pipes (seven to each of the seven lamps). The container received its supplies of oil from two olive trees with fruitful branches. In the normal course, the olive oil was extracted by crushing the olive berries, but in this case the bowl was supplied direct from the trees through two additional golden pipes, which ran from the trees to the bowl. There was no intermediate extraction of the oil from the fruit: no human agency was required.

Zechariah frankly acknowledged that he did not understand the symbols, and the interpreting angel accordingly explained that God's work was not accomplished by human might or power (cf. Hos. 1:7), but by the Holy Spirit, of whom the olive oil was such an apt type. It was also tacitly implied that even the gift of the Holy Spirit and the outpouring of His power are not dependent upon the efforts of the individual: human endeavour is superfluous and inappropriate. The Spirit is given without measure to those who are prepared to receive Him unhinderedly and to abandon themselves to His control. Nothing is accomplished in the service of God merely by human ability: we are dependent entirely upon the Holy Spirit. 'Not by might, nor by power, but by my Spirit,' said God. David Baron (op. cit., p. 137) says that the word 'might' is one which also 'means a host or army and may mean "the strength of many"'. The word 'power', however, 'stands for that of one man. The two might be taken to express human strength and power of every description – physical, mental and moral – individual or the combined strength of the multitude'. The work of God is not accomplished in human strength. 'Not many wise men after the flesh, not many mighty, not many noble, are called,' wrote the apostle Paul, 'but God has chosen the foolish things of the world to confound the wise; and God has chosen the weak things of the world to confound the things which are mighty; and base things of the world, and things which are despised, has God chosen, and things which are not, to bring to nought things that are: that no flesh should glory in His presence' (Cor. 1:26–29). This is the constant lesson which God's servant is to learn: he is completely insufficient and inadequate: his sufficiency is of God.

It mattered not if difficulties seemed to be mountains high and completely insuperable, if defence against political attacks and intrigues seemed impossible, and if the machinations of the surrounding nations seemed destined to hamper the work still further. The power of the Holy Spirit would level the mountain to a plain before Zerubbabel, the builder of God's temple. Schemes and intrigues counted for nothing with Jehovah. When He blew upon the enemy's plans, they disintegrated and disappeared. The same power is available to the Christian today. God is his sufficiency. Mountains disappear and difficulties vanish at the breath of the Divine Spirit. Chambers (op. cit., p. 43) says, 'In the sixteenth century one man entered the lists against the Antichristian corruptions of the time . . . in the issue one half of Europe was emancipated from the papal yoke.' One man indwelt and empowered by the Holy Spirit is greater than an army.

In the previous vision, the Servant of Jehovah had been referred to, *inter alia*, as a stone – evidently the headstone and the crowning stone which completed the building. The angel now declared that, in due time, Zerubbabel would bring forth the headstone to crown the reconstruction of the temple. Then the shoutings of builders and people would be heard, 'Grace, grace to it!' or, as another renders it, 'What gracefulness it has!' or 'How perfectly graceful it is!' When Solomon's temple was being built, every stone was prepared in the quarry below and shaped for its appointed place in the building, so that no sound of hammer or chisel was heard on the site above (1 Kings 6:7). The stones were brought out to harden in the sun and the workmen took from the piles as they built the temple. Tradition says that, among the stones one day the builders came across one of different size and shape, for which there seemed no place in the building. It was consequently cast aside, rejected by the builders. When the darkness suddenly fell at night, they would sometimes stumble over the rejected stone and it was often referred to as the stumbling-stone. In due course, however, the work reached its final stages and the appropriate stone was sought to fill the place of the head of the corner. No other stone filled the vacant place, but the workmen presently brought forth the stone they had rejected and over which they had stumbled, with glad shoutings of 'Grace, grace to it', for the rejected stone exactly fitted the vacant place for the topstone – the place of glory and honour. Whether or not there is any substance in the tradition, our Lord certainly referred the figure to Himself (Matt. 21:42–44; Luke 20:17, 18). He was the One whom the nation rejected and over whom they had stumbled, but one day He will be acknowledged as the worthy One and the crown and headship will be His.

The rebuilding of the temple was nearing completion and God declared that Zerubbabel, who had laid the foundation, would see the last stone – the headstone – fitted into its place. He would complete the building. Since it was to be completed in the lifetime of the one who had laid the foundation, it was evident that God was not going to allow the work to drag on interminably. The promise not only guaranteed the completion, but virtually declared its imminence. When the work was finished in such difficult and adverse circumstances, incontrovertible proof would have been furnished that the message which the people had received through Zechariah had originated with Jehovah – that He had sent His messenger (either the interpreting angel or the prophet).

Some of those who had watched the rebuilding of the temple had evidently poured scorn and ridicule on the work. It was not an elaborate or ornate building that was being erected and was certainly not comparable for splendour with its predecessor. The critics evidently declared that if it was not deserving of respect. It was an age, they declared, when relatively little was accomplished: it was a day of small things. But Jehovah interposed again with the question, 'Who has despised the day of small things?' It was not for others to estimate the value or importance of the work. God alone assesses the work at its true value and the final judgement rests with Him. How often today the Lord's servant is discouraged by the depreciation of his service by those who establish themselves as critics. God has called His servants to undertake a work for Him. Others may deem it of little value or importance and the work may seem small even to those engaged upon it. But who are we to judge? He that is faithful in little is also faithful in much. Even if it seems a day in which little is accomplished. God's question is still pertinent, 'Who has despised the day of small things?' The trivial task upon which we are employed may be the key to the whole of a great project. Who dare despise what God has entrusted to us?

Some had despised the day of small things, but the Divine message declared that there would be rejoicing (whether by the critics or by the seven eyes of Jehovah is not clearly indicated) when the plummet was seen in the hand of Zerubbabel. Perowne (op. cit., p. 87) renders verse 10, 'For who has despised the day of small things? For (seeing that) these seven eyes of Jehovah, which run to and fro throughout all the earth, shall rejoice to see the plummet in the hand of Zerubbabel,' and pertinently remarks, 'Since then God beholds the progress of the work with joy and favour, who will venture to despise it?' Those eyes which ranged through the whole earth and detected every happening, and which were focused upon the stone symbol of Jehovah's Servant in chapter 3, now found joy in the completed temple and the provision again of an earthly dwelling place for the Eternal, where His people could have communion with Him.

The plummet was a string from which was suspended a heavy weight and it was used as a plumbline to ensure that the stones and walls of the temple were in perfect alignment. The fact that it was in the hand of Zerubbabel was an indication that he was actively engaged in ensuring the completion of the temple and its perfect precision.

The prophet was, however, still without an explanation of the lampstand and the trees and he asked for enlightenment. The angel then explained that the two olive trees symbolized the two anointed ones (or 'sons of oil'), who stood by the Lord of the whole earth. Only kings and priests were anointed, and it is usually suggested that the reference was to Zerubbabel and Joshua, the civil and religious leaders, who were the medium of Divine contact with the people. It was their responsibility to ensure that the Divine will in civil and religious matters was implemented by the nation and, in the purpose of God, they were set apart for this purpose. In Rev. 11:4 the two witnesses of a future day are described as 'the two olive trees and the two lampstands standing before the God of the earth', clearly a reference to Zech. 4. They may also be symbolic of spiritual powers. The antitype of Zerubbabel and Joshua is, of course, to be found in the Messiah, who combines both offices in Himself (see Zech. 6:13), and is the source of all sufficiency for His people.

The branches poured a copious supply of oil (symbolized as liquid gold in verse 12) into the bowl through two pipes. The angel's interpretation in the closing verse of the chapter did not distinguish between the pipes and the trees, but virtually implied that both were symbolic of the 'two anointed ones'. Certainly Messiah is to be the source and means of supply to Israel – as, of course, He is today to the Christian.

CHAPTER 8

A Holy People

Zech. 3 described the cleansing of the priesthood and provided the nation with an assurance of access to and communion with Jehovah. Zech. 4 showed the means by which sanctification and spiritual enduement were obtained and emphasized the complete inadequacy of all human effort. Zech. 5 is concerned with the cleansing and sanctification of the nation and the land and, by inference, stresses the Divine intolerance of sin in the individual or the nation. Sin must be judged and iniquity must be removed. God is infinitely holy, and His people must be holy too. Those, who harboured their sin and refused to put it away, must suffer under the hand of God. There is no place for the impenitent and the recalcitrant. It has been suggested, with some justification, that the inexorable judgement of sin and sinners portrayed in the sixth vision, while applying in the first instance to the returned exiles, has an even greater pertinence to the period of Christ's theocratic kingdom, when He will rule the nations with a rod of iron and dash the wicked to pieces like the smashing of a potter's vessel (Ps. 2:9). The immediate application, however, was to those who had now returned to the land under Joshua and Zerubbabel.

The description of the sixth vision was brief.

'Then I lifted up my eyes again and saw and behold, a flying roll. And he said to me, What do you see? And I answered, I see a flying roll: the length of it is twenty cubits, and the breadth of it ten cubits. Then he said to me, This is the curse that is going forth over the face of the whole land: for every one who steals shall be cut off as on this side according to it; and every one who swears shall be cut off as on that side according to it. I will cause it to issue forth, says Jehovah of hosts, and it shall enter into the house of the thief and into the house of him who swears falsely by my name: and it shall abide in the midst of his house, and shall consume it with its timber and its stones' (5:1–4).

The vision that now crossed the prophet's eyes was a remarkable one. He saw an enormous roll, like an expanded banner, flying swiftly through the air, and evidently bearing writing on both sides. 'Books were written,' to quote one expositor, 'on long sheets or rolls made of papyrus, a sort of paper made of the pith of the papyrus plant, the paper reed. The pith was cut into strips, layers of which were laid crosswise and pressed or glued together to form the writing paper. Sometimes both sides were used (cf. Rev. 5:1).' Sir George Adam Smith (op cit., p. 301) however, considers that the roll was not of papyrus since Zechariah used 'the ordinary Hebrew name for the rolls of skin or parchment,' but the material used matters little. A scroll was normally wound around a rod (sometimes one was used for each end), but the one seen by Zechariah was obviously unrolled so that all might read its contents. It seems clear that a table of the law was written on each side.

The roll was of an extraordinary size – twenty cubits by ten cubits, or roughly ten yards by five yards, the same size as the tabernacle in the wilderness (Exod. 26:15–25) and also the same size as the porch of Solomon's temple (1 Kings 6:3), where the law was normally read. There is possibly the implication that judgement would be meted out in accordance with God's holiness and in accordance with the measure of the sanctuary.

The angel described the roll as the curse that was going forth over the whole land, since it conveyed a curse upon the transgressor of the law inscribed upon it. Smend regards as relevant the practice in ancient times for curses to be written on pieces of paper and for these to be sent down the wind into the houses of those against whom they were directed, but Smith sees a picture of birds of prey as more appropriate. The central commandment from each of the two tables of the decalogue was selected as illustrative of the whole, plainly implying that the breach of one commandment constituted a breaking of the whole law and rendered the individual a transgressor (see also Jas. 2:10). From the first table, stealing was selected as 'representing all violations of the rights of one's fellow men'. From the second table, swearing or perjury was chosen as 'representing all sins directed specifically against God and His holy name.'

The one who transgressed the law thereby brought himself under its curse (Deut. 27:26; Gal. 3:10), and the flying roll, therefore, became the vehicle of the curse to be judicially laid upon the guilty. Every infraction of the law was to be relentlessly punished and there was no suggestion of mercy or leniency. The time for repentance had passed and the sinner was to be 'cut off' – or possibly 'purged out' of the land. The nation and the land must be cleansed of every contamination, and the sinner must be dealt with in unmitigated justice. The minatory character of the vision was in startling and salutary contrast to the consolatory terms of the preceding visions, but God's holiness was at stake.

The roll would enter the house of the guilty one, declared Jehovah, and, by inference, ferret out his wrongdoing and reveal his sin. It would convict him of the evil of his ways, thoughts and speech, and it would abide in his house to effect the complete and unrelieved destruction of every stone and timber. Nothing would be preserved. Such was the unquenchable fire of God's holiness. He would by no means clear the guilty. The curse would abide upon the house. Perowne (op. cit., pp. 89, 90) refers, 'in illustration of the curse abiding till it has accomplished its mission, the story of Glaucus (Herodotus vi 86), who consulted the oracle as to whether he was at liberty to perjure himself, and retain for his own use a sum of money which had been committed to his trust. The response was that though such a course would be for his present gain, "yet an oath hath a nameless son, headless and footless, yet swift in pursuit till he seize and destroy the whole race and house". And accordingly, though Glaucus restored the money and asked for forgiveness for the thought of his heart, it was observed that, since to design evil was to incur the guilt of executing it, his family became extinct.'

The message of the vision is not without its significance for the present day. The standard of holiness which God required from His people has not been lowered, and even the Christian needs the constant reminder of the apostle John that the one who claims to belong to Christ should conduct himself as the Master did and that the one who commits sin is of the devil (1 John 2:6; 3:8). Our Lord's own prayer was that His people might be sanctified through the truth (John 17:17). The disregard of business morality, the laxity in general conduct and morals, the association with the questionable things of the world, the frequent impurity of thought and word are completely irreconcilable with the unblemished purity of Christ. In view of the price paid at Calvary for the removal of the believer's defilement, how can he possibly give rein to desires and actions which so obviously contaminate mind and life? God cannot tolerate sin and impurity and, if there is a deliberate refusal to put away the unclean thing, the flying roll may still enter the house and wreak complete destruction of all that has been treasured. We ignore the implicit warning of the vision at our peril. T. V. Moore (*Zechariah*, p. 80) says, 'There is something most vivid and appalling in this image of the hovering curse. It flies viewless and resistless, poising like a falcon over her prey, breathing a ruin the most dire and desolating, and when the blind and hardened offender opens his door to his ill-gotten gains, this mysterious roll, with its fire-tracery of wrath, enters into his habitation, and fastening upon his cherished idols, begins its dread work of retribution, and ceases not until the fabric of his guilty life has been totally and irremediably consumed.'

If the sixth vision was concerned with the sin of the individual, the seventh was directed to the cleansing of the nation from what has been termed the 'ungodly secularism and intense commercial preoccupation' which had gripped them. The message was presented in a picturesque form.

'Then the angel who talked with me came forth, and said to me, Lift up now your eyes and see what it is that is going forth. And I said, What is it? And he said, This is the ephah that is going forth. He said, moreover, This is their appearance through all the land. And behold, a circle of lead was lifted up: and this is a woman sitting in the middle of the ephah. And he said, This is wickedness. And he thrust her down into the middle of the ephah; and he cast the weight of lead upon its mouth. Then I raised my eyes and saw, and behold, there came forth two women, and the wind was in their wings; for they had wings like the wings of a stork; and they lifted up the ephah between earth and heaven. Then said I to the angel who talked with me, Whither do these bear the ephah? And he said to me, To build a house for it in the land of Shinar, and when it is established, it shall be caused to rest there on its own base' (5:5–11).

As part of the Divine plan for the removal of sin and uncleanness from the land, God was about to take further action. Zechariah saw an ephah, a large container, adequate to hold a bushel of corn or ten omers (Exod. 16:36). It would not be large enough to hold a human being of average size, but, as indicated later, one was held therein. The angel explained that the ephah was a representation of the sinful state of the people throughout the land of Judah.

The ephah was an appropriate symbol of trade or commerce. As a pastoral people the Jews had little experience of the soulless self-centredness of commercialism until they had been exiled in Babylon, but there it had gripped them to such an extent that it became an outstanding characteristic of them on their return to their own land. Unger (op. cit., p. 93) says, 'It was the new principle with which the Jews had become imbued in Babylon, and which had exercised such a potent formative influence over them throughout the centuries and will continue to do so until it is removed from them at the advent of their Messiah.' Commerce is not, of course, wrong in itself, but the temptations to which Judah had been exposed had led to an inordinate obsession with material prosperity and an insatiable greed for gain. Laetsch (op. cit., p. 433) points out that 'the Lord demands a just ephah, full measure, integrity and honesty in selling and buying in all business and judicial transactions (Lev. 19:35 f.; Deut, 25:4 f.; Ezek. 45:9 ff.; Mic. 6:10–15)'. Commercial morality was disappearing and the mercenary spirit was affecting every business transaction. In the words of another prophet, they were 'making the ephah small and the shekel great and falsifying the balances by deceit' (Amos 8:5). The amoral and incurable cupidity and unlawful practices of the market-place were spreading throughout the country and were even affecting judicial decisions in their courts.

The prevalent condition was due not only to the unfortunate commercial practices with which Judah had become acquainted in Babylon, but at least partially to the low state of morality generally in Babylonia. Of the city itself, a Roman historian declared that 'nothing could be more corrupt than its morals, nothing more fitted to excite and allure to immoderate pleasures. The rites of hospitality were polluted by the grossest and most shameless lusts. Money dissolved every tie, whether of kindred, respect or esteem. Drunkenness and the grossest immoralities were practised in public.' 'This is their appearance (or possibly "their iniquity") throughout all the land', declared the angel. The whole of the country was affected. There was a need for the cleansing of the returned exiles and their land.

The conditions of the present day are not very dissimilar. Even Christians seem to be completely obsessed by an inordinate and unhealthy desire for gain, and to be prepared to sacrifice any principles for personal benefit. The same grasping spirit, the same ruthless endeavour to improve or to increase wealth, the same insensate desire for the material rather than the spiritual, all indicate the extent to which Babylonian 'commercialism' has affected those who belong to Christ. If there was a need for a purging from wrong desires and motives in Zechariah's day, there is a comparable need today.

As the ephah drew nearer, the prophet saw that a lid (described as a talent or circle of lead), which had apparently closed it, was being pushed up from within and that a woman contained within was evidently trying to escape. This, the angel informed him, was wickedness, i.e. the personification of unrighteous actions and intentions; sin was naturally unwilling to accept restriction and was endeavouring to secure liberty to roam at will. But the angel pushed the woman back into the confined space of the ephah and slammed the leaden lid upon the mouth of the container. A talent was the largest measure of weight used by the Jews and was equivalent to just over 66 lb. or 30 kg. Baron (op. cit., p. 164) says that 'the talent, with which she carries on her unrighteous trade, becomes the heavy weight by which she is held down till she is landed safely in her own place!'

The point of the vision, however, was not the governmental repression of the woman or the restraint of wickedness in the land, nor even its punishment or destruction, but rather its complete removal from the land. Two women, with huge wings like those of a stork (an unclean bird – see Lev. 11:19; Deut. 14:18) outstretched for flight as if their pinions already felt the power of the wind, seized the ephah and its evil occupant and flew away with it between earth and heaven. The wind was not merely to increase their velocity; carrying away by the wind is consistently regarded in the Scriptures as indicative of judgement (e.g. Job. 27:20, 22; 30:22; Isa. 41:16; 7:13; 64:6).

The two women have been interpreted in a variety of ways. Many deem them to be instruments of God's justice and their removal of the ephah as an action taken at Divine direction, although there is no indication of this in the record. Others, *per contra*, regard the two women as evil agents who acted to deliver the imprisoned woman from the impending vengeance which seemed imminent. David Baron, who is followed by M. F. Unger in this, inclines to the second view. He says (op. cit., p. 166) that the two women 'may be apostate Christianity united in the last days to apostate Judaism, and both given over to the worship of Mammon, on which the power of the ephah is based' or that symbolic reference may be to 'the civil and ecclesiastic powers. . . . The two women here may, perhaps, be meant to signify civil government broken loose, even outwardly, from every acknowledgement of God (and, therefore, an instrument in the hand of lawlessness), and a corrupt antichristian and antitheistic priesthood – both Jewish and Gentile – ready to unite as spouses and protectors to a system which, though as yet not so regarded, even by the elect, is characterized by God as "the wickedness").' This seems somewhat fanciful. T. V. Moore (op. cit., p. 84) argues that 'they symbolized the messengers of God's wrath that should desolate Judea and banish the people. They were to carry it into Shinar, which is here the symbol for an enemy's country, and not the exact country to which they were to be exiled . . .weighed down like lead with judicial blindness, stupidity, darkness, and hardness of heart.' In other words, he sees the long *diaspora* of nineteen centuries symbolized in the carrying away, but this is hardly tenable since the context is the cleansing of the land from that which defiled it. Commercial inequity and amorality had seized hold of the people: the vision showed that this kind of unrighteousness or wickedness must be removed from the land before the ultimate blessing of God was experienced. It was not the people but their iniquity that was to be removed. Whether the instruments used were themselves evil characters or not, is not of great importance. Ungodly nations and evil men have been frequently used by the Almighty to achieve His purposes.

The perplexed prophet asked where the ephah was being borne and was informed that the women were carrying it away to build an abode for it in the land of Shinar and when it was settled there, it would rest on its own base. Keil takes the view that Shinar was not intended here to denote a particular geographical location, but rather as an ideal designation of the sphere of ungodliness. Smith says, 'Shinar, from its earliest days, was a land of open rebellion against God. Throughout Scripture it is symbolic of wickedness and opposition to God. Shinar is the symbol of Satan's kingdom of wickedness.' Kelly (op. cit., p. 457) remarks, 'From Shinar religious corruption came, and thither it must go, forcibly and swiftly carried off: such is the measure meted by Jehovah . . . it is the idolatrous evil of the Jews derived from and sent back to Babylon.' Certainly Shinar was the origin of paganism as well as of the first attempt to establish a world empire (see pp. 91, 92 of *God's Programme of the Ages*, by F. A. Tatford). The wickedness described in the vision originated in Babylon: it has infected the Jewish race for centuries as with a virus. But the day is coming when they will be purged of this spirit and the evil be removed. It is only appropriate that symbolically it should be returned to the place of its origin.

An abode was to be built for the ephah in its own land of Shinar. An anonymous writer's comments are pertinent. He says, 'While iniquity is away from its base, it is iniquity in mystery. But once returned, its house is built: it is settled, no more to be moved till judgement crush it: it is expanded, and its manifestation is to meet and receive the full wrath of God.' Zechariah's vision merely foretells the removal of the evil from the land of Israel, but the apocalyptic writer discloses the ultimate doom which befalls the whole of this evil system in the day of Divine judgement (Rev. 18).

There is obviously a lesson for the believer of the present age. One writer expresses it succinctly, 'Whilst even the justified and sanctified believer needs daily cleansing and forgiveness, wickedness and manifest rebellion against God could not be tolerated. It must be removed by removing the wicked man or men' (cf. 1 Cor. 5:5; 11:30).

CHAPTER 9

The Four Chariots

Zechariah's long night was nearly over and the last vision now broke upon his gaze. 'The first vision and the eighth,' says Barnes (op. cit., p. 51), 'form together the framework in which the whole section (1:7–6:8) is set. The one appropriately begins, the other appropriately closes the series of visions. Neither is a theophany (a revelation of God) but each stands instead of a theophany. . . . In the first the angel of Jehovah appears and converses through the veil with Jehovah Himself. In the last the gate between heaven and earth is opened and the "four spirits of heaven" in the guise of chariots come forth.' The account of the vision was as follows.

'And once more I lifted up my eyes and saw and, behold, there came out four chariots from between the two mountains; and the mountains were mountains of brass. In the first chariot were red horses; and in the second chariot black horses; and in the third chariot white horses; and in the fourth chariot grisled and bay horses. Then I answered and said to the angel who talked to me, What are these, my lord? And the angel answered and said to me, These are the four spirits of the heavens, which go forth from standing before the Lord of all the earth. The chariot in which are the black horses is going forth into the land of the north, and the white went forth to the land which was behind them; and the grisled went forth toward the land of the south. And the bay went forth, and sought to go that they might walk to and fro through the earth. And he said, Get you hence, walk to and fro through the earth. So they walked to and fro through the earth. Then cried he upon me and spoke to me, saying, Behold, these that go toward the north country have caused my spirit to have rest in the north country' (6:1–8).

Judgement always begins with the house of God, but it then reaches out to those around. Having dealt with the sin in Judah and having removed wickedness from the land, Jehovah proceeded with the execution of judgement in a wider field. 'The wrath of God,' says one writer, 'is not a caprice or an impulse, but the steady, uniform, eternal element of His being. He is necessarily "of purer eyes than to behold evil".' His abhorrence of sin must consequently demonstrate itself in the judgement of the guilty. In the first vision, the reconnaissance troop reported that the whole earth was at rest and tranquil, and Jehovah intimated that His anger would break out upon the nations which had oppressed His people and were themselves enjoying peace and quiet. In the eighth vision the threat was symbolically fulfilled and judgement was poured out – at least, in figure. The eight visions, therefore, virtually formed a circle.

Zechariah saw four chariots issue forth from between two mountains of brass or copper. The use of the definite article indicates that the mountains were well known, and expositors have suggested that they were either Zion and Moriah, or Zion and Olivet, and that the chariots would rush through the valley of Jehoshaphat on their appointed mission. Joel 3:2 reveals that this valley will be the site of the future judgement of the nations and presumably has reference to the period described in Zechariah. Some writers, however, have taken the view that the two indestructible mountains form the gate towers guarding the entrance to the palace of the Supreme Ruler of the universe, from which the messengers of judgement would issue at the Divine command. Others have argued that the mountains refer to the great spiritual powers or agencies, which overthrow empires and shake the destiny of nations, but this view can hardly be sustained because the judgement came by the medium of the chariots and not by the mountains. Brass or copper (or military bronze) is usually regarded as figurative of judgement (e.g. the brazen serpent of Num. 21:9 and the brazen altar of Exod. 27:2), but it would be unwise to regard the mountains as anything more than the gates through which judgement came.

The interpreting angel explained that the four chariots represented the four spirits of the heavens, which issued forth from the immediate presence of the Almighty. Baron (op. cit., p. 175) considers that they should be interpreted 'either as ideal appearances, personifying the forces and providential acts which God often uses in carrying out His judgements on the earth, or . . . angelic beings, or heavenly powers – those invisible messengers of His'. The number four may perhaps indicate the universality of the Divine judgements. The identification of the chariots with the four great empires of Dan. 2 and 7 or with the four sore judgements of Ezek. 14:21 can scarcely be accepted. As one writer remarks, the picture is not of the great Gentile world powers, but rather 'the overthrow and judgement of these by means of invisible heavenly powers appointed of God as a necessary precursor to the establishment of Messiah's kingdom, and the blessing of Israel, which is symbolically set forth to the prophet in this last vision'. God had declared in the second vision that the four artificers whom He sent would terrify the Gentile nations and destroy their power because of what they had done to Judah.

The chariots were drawn by horses of various colours. The first had red horses, the symbol of war and bloodshed (cf. Rev. 6:4); the second had black horses, the figure of famine and death (cf. Rev. 6:5, 6); the third had white horses, which some have identified with the peaceful conquest of Rev. 6:2; the fourth chariot had grisled and bay horses (or possibly 'dappled and strong'), perhaps symbolic of plague and pestilence (Rev. 6:8). The Eternal uses His own intruments for the destruction of His foes.

The second chariot, with its black horses, was about to drive forth on its punitive expedition against the north country. The north was the direction from which the most serious invasions of Israel and Judah always came; Assyria, Babylonia and Medo-Persia were all located to the north of the land. Jehovah's spirit had been unquiet, because the nations which had afflicted His people were enjoying the fruits of their ravages with impunity and it is specifically recorded that the avengers who swept against the north thereby quieted His spirit. It was in the north that apostasy first broke out in human history and it was there that the foundations of the first world empire were laid by rebels against the Almighty. It was under the yoke of the northern power that many of God's people were at that moment groaning. His anger, therefore, rested first and most fully upon the north and, not until the objects of His wrath had suffered the determined chastisement, was His mind at peace again. The use by the prophetic word of anthropomorphic expressions in relation to God was, of course, only to convey to human minds an understanding, however faint, of the Divine actions. The judgement of the north was not restricted to what is now past history: it patently anticipated the events of the future to which Daniel referred in Dan. 11:36–45, and confirmed the complete destruction to be meted out upon the northern foe.

The chariot in which were the white horses, according to the A.V., followed the black horses to the north, but a more probable rendering is that they 'went forth to the land which was behind them', i.e. to the west. As Barnes says (in loc.), 'An Eastern in reckoning the points of the compass faces the rising sun; consequently behind him is the west.' In the day of Israel's future extremity, it seems evident that the land will suffer invasions from every point of the compass. If, as seems implied by Dan. 9:27, there is to be a treaty between Israel and a western group of nations, with a guarantee, *inter alia*, of protection from invasion by the northern power, the events described in the closing verses of Dan. 11 would obviously invoke an intervention by the western powers. But their character will be as godless as that of the northern power (see Rev. 13:1–8) and the judgement of God will inevitably fall upon them also (Rev. 19:20). It is thought by some students of prophecy that the rider on the white horse of Rev. 6:2 is to be identified with the first beast of Rev. 13, i.e. the ultimate dictator of the ten western countries: this would certainly provide a link with Zech. 6:6.

The grisled or dappled horses drove southwards. To the south of Judah lay the ancient land of Egypt, which, for centuries, was the foe of Israel and Judah. It is evident from Dan. 11 that the antagonism of Egypt will yet burst into active opposition, and Ezek. 35 and Ps. 83 indicate that the permanent hatred of the Edomites (or of the Arab nations which have succeeded them and the Ishmaelites) will flare up, presumably at the same time. For the trouble inflicted upon God's people in the past and for all that is still presaged, the punitive hand of the Almighty will rest upon the land of the south.

The bay or strong horses may be identical with the red horses of the first chariot, since these are not otherwise referred to when the action commences. The Peshitta or Syrian version of the first or second century A.D. and also the Greek translation made by the Jewish proselyte Aquila in the second century A.D. both translate the word as 'red' instead of 'bay'. On the other hand, the word 'bay' (or 'strong') is used in verse 3 as one of the two appellatives for the horses of the fourth chariot. Baron argues that the omission of any reference to the red horses after verse 2 is due to the fact that Babylonia had already been destroyed by Medo-Persia and that further punitive action was, therefore, unnecessary, but this explanation seems rather weak. These bay (or strong) or red horses petitioned (i.e. their riders did) to be allowed to traverse the earth – obviously to deal with any other hostile forces. Barnes (op. cit., p. 53) writes, 'The strong horses are those which are assigned the task of patrolling; their function is to keep Judah safe.' In answer to their request, the Divine commission was given to go and walk to and fro through the earth (or possibly 'the land').

It was essential (and still is) that judgement should be unleashed upon the Gentile nations preparatory to the setting up of the theocratic kingdom at the coming of the Messiah. So the messengers of Divine vengeance issue forth. 'A voice says, "Go", and they at once start out on their punitive expedition. As they rush by, Zechariah hears a voice above the rattling of the chariots. It is the voice of Jehovah, speaking of Himself. The chariots going towards the north will satisfy Him by allotting His enemies the full measure of their well-deserved punishment.' He had been sore displeased, but now He was at rest. In pursuing their own course, the nations leave God out of their deliberations, and act as if the Almighty did not exist. But the Supreme Ruler of the universe has not abdicated. He still fills the eternal throne in the celestial heights and takes account of every act, thought and word – not only of the individual, but of the nations of earth. One day He will once more intervene in human affairs and display His absolute righteousness in the chastisement of the guilty – both nations and men.

Moore's comment is worth quoting *in extenso*. He says (op. cit., pp. 90–92), 'how striking the fulfilment of this threatening when we remember the circumstances under which it was made. Could the haughty nobles of Babylon, in the gorgeousness of its magnificence and the pride of its power, have heard the threatening of this obscure Jew, amidst the ruins of Jerusalem, with what derision and contempt would they have treated the threat! The anathema that was so feebly uttered against the mightiest and richest city of the world, to the eye of sense seemed like the ravings of lunacy. Yet that feeble whisper was the uttered voice of Jehovah, and the elements of ruin in their remotest lurking-place heard the summons and began to come forth. Slowly and silently did they come up to this dread work, and yet surely and resistlessly, until the glory of these high palaces was dimmed, and the magnificence of these gardens and temples was covered, and now the winds whistle through the reeds of the Euphrates, where Babylon then sat in her pride: and loveliness; desolation and death are stationed there; the sentinel witnesses of the truth that His word returns not to Him void, that His spirit is quieted in the land of the north. Egypt also was yet proud and powerful. Memphis still sat in her queenly pride by the old and solemn Nile, and Thebes still retained the glory of that wonderful architecture that yet amazed the world. They had stood thus from the hoariest antiquity, and how should it be thought that, at the bidding of the descendant of an Egyptian slave, this ancient magnificence would depart. Yet this bidding was obeyed, and wave after wave of desolation swept over this haughty land, until now the pyramids, the sphinxes and the temples of the mighty past but mock the degenerate baseness of the mournful present. Thus was it later in history with Greece and Rome, thus shall it be with guilty and godless Europe, thus shall it be with every enemy of the Church, who attempts to thwart the designs of God in the world. But as the final development of this vision of judgement was to be subsequent to the completion of the threatened punishment of the Jews, we know that it has not yet received its last and mightiest fulfilment. That shall take place only when the Lord . . . shall be revealed from heaven in flaming fire, taking vengeance on all His enemies. Then, and not until then, shall this vision receive its last, its most terrible and complete fulfilment.'

Thus the night of the eight visions concluded.

CHAPTER 10

Joshua's Coronation

The visions of the long night were over and were succeeded (not necessarily immediately) by a symbolic action obviously taken in full view of a number of spectators. It is desirable to understand the circumstances of the people in Judea at the time in order to appreciate the full significance of the incident. We can do little better than quote Barnes again on this point. He says (op. cit., p. 54) that the people 'were sharply divided into two sections: those who had had experience of captivity and those who had not. The latter, the remnant left in Judea by the Chaldeans, being deprived of their best leaders, were very weak in religious and national feeling; they had begun, in fact, to be absorbed by their heathen neighbours. In Babylonia, on the contrary, exile from Jerusalem tended to increase the devotion of the exiles to their city. So it was that many responded to the edict by which Cyrus invited them to rebuild the temple; they proved their zeal for their religion and country by breaking up their homes in Babylonia and returning to a half-ruined province which was little ready to receive them. In Judea these men and their descendants were known as *Bene-golah*, 'children of captivity' or (more briefly) as the *Golah*, "captivity"'. They regarded themselves as distinct from and superior to those who had never experienced exile. The incident now described by Zechariah concerned the visit to Jerusalem of a Jewish family ('the household of Josiah the son of Zephaniah') with gifts for the work of the temple.

'And the word of Jehovah came to me saying, Take men of the *golah*, even their leaders, of the families of Tobijah and Jedaiah, and enter in the same day and go in unto the household of Josiah the son of Zephaniah, who have come from Babylon. Then take of them silver and gold and make crowns, and set them on the head of Joshua, the son of Josedech, the high priest. And speak to him, saying, Thus speaks Jehovah of hosts, saying, Behold a man whose name is the Branch; and he shall shoot forth from under him, and he shall build the temple of Jehovah. Even he shall build the temple of Jehovah, and he shall bear the glory, and shall sit and rule on his throne; and he shall be a priest on his throne, and the counsel of peace shall be between them both. And the crown shall be for health to Tobijah and Jedaiah and for favour to the son of Zephaniah, for a memorial in the temple of Jehovah. And they that are far off shall come and build in the temple of Jehovah, and you shall know that Jehovah of hosts has sent me to you. And it shall come to pass if you will diligently obey the voice of Jehovah your God' (6:9–15).

In the translation of verse 2 we have followed Dr. W. E. Barnes, who takes the view that the household of Josiah, the son of Zephaniah, had returned as pilgrims from Babylon and that, on the day of their arrival, the prophet was instructed to take certain leaders (the word 'Heldai' is used by the Septuagint, for example, as a common noun with the meaning of 'rulers') of the *golah*, men of the families of Tobijah and Jedaiah, to welcome them. The A.V. regards 'Heldai' as a proper name and it also (as does the R.S.V.) incorrectly places the clause, 'who are come from Babylon', after Jedaiah instead of after 'Zephaniah', where it correctly belongs (and is so placed by the R.V.). Moore, on the other hand, correctly places the clause at the end, but renders the verse, 'Take of (them of) the captivity, of Heldai of Tobijah, of Jedaiah, and go thou in that day, and go to the house of Josiah the son of Zephaniah, who (all) have come from Babylon.' The matter is not of great importance, but it seems more probable that Barnes' rendering is the most correct and also the most appropriate. 'Helem' in verse 14 is usually regarded as another name for 'Heldai', but it could more correctly be translated as 'recovery' or 'health'. In the same verse, 'Hen' is regarded as an alternative for 'Josiah', but there is no justification for rendering it in any other way than 'favour' or 'kindness'.

The exiles in Babylon had heard of the resumption of the work of rebuilding the temple and doubtless a number of pilgrims came to Jerusalem from time to time. At any rate, the family of Josiah came with their gifts for the temple. With some of the leaders of the *golah*, Zechariah went immediately to visit the family. Acting under the direction of God, he took silver and gold from the gifts the exiles had brought and, with these materials, constructed crowns or, more probably, a crown composed of circlets of gold and silver. This he placed upon the brow of Joshua, the high priest. Joshua of course, had no claim to regal dignity and never, in fact, became the civil or political ruler of Judah. He was not a scion of the royal tribe, as Zerubbabel was, but was a member of the priestly tribe. It was clear, therefore, that his coronation was symbolic and not personal and this is confirmed by the following verses. It might have been expected that Zerubbabel, as the civil leader, would have received the honour rather than Joshua, but as Unger points out (op. cit., p. 112), the crowning of Zerubbabel as 'an heir of the Davidic dynasty would have been misleading, pointing to a re-establishment of the Davidic kingdom, which was not the divine purpose at that moment'.

Joshua was not acknowledged as king of Judah or of Israel, but he was told, in effect, that he was figurative of 'a man whose name is the Branch'. As already indicated in chapter 6, this was used particularly of the Messiah, and Joshua's coronation was obviously prefigurative of that of God's chosen King in a coming day. It was predicted that that One would 'shoot forth from under Him', or 'grow up out of His place' (A.V.). In other words, He would be of lowly and humble origin (cf. Isa. 53:2). Certainly this was true of the Messiah at His first advent. He lived in humble circumstances and probably worked as a village carpenter; His disciples were relative nonentities; during His public ministry He was dependent upon the charity and hospitality of others; He had nowhere to lay His head; on the cross the seamless robe of the Palestinian peasant – His last garment – was taken from Him; His body ultimately lay in a borrowed tomb. The words uttered to Zechariah were clearly true of the One who came.

The temple was being rebuilt now, but God declared that this One would build the temple of Jehovah. The temple of Zerubbabel was, therefore, regarded as only a temporary building. The building of the true temple was reserved for the Messiah himself. This cannot refer, as some expositors have argued, to our Lord's statement that, if the temple (of His body) was destroyed, He would raise it up in three days (John 2:19–21), nor to the spiritual temple which is the Divine habitation today (Eph. 2:21, 22). Nor is it possible to regard the prophecy as relating to Zerubbabel and the completion of the temple which was then under construction, since the Branch was not a title pertinent to Zerubbabel. The words clearly anticipated the building of a literal temple and presumably relate to the millennial temple described by Ezekiel (Ezek. 40–42; Isa. 2:2, 3).

Jehovah declared that the One who was to build the temple would also 'bear the glory'. Haggai had averred that the temple would be filled with glory and that the latter glory (rather than the 'glory of this latter house') would be greater than the former glory (Hag. 2:7, 9). Since Christ, who is the effulgence of God's glory, will enter the millennial temple to dwell among His people (Ezek. 43:2; cf. 1:26–28; Rev. 21:23), it is obvious that the future glory will be incomparably greater than the shekinah of old. But the expression used signifies 'royal majesty' rather than 'glory'. Unger says that the Hebrew word *hodh*, which is here translated 'glory', 'is used almost exclusively of the divine splendour' (Ps. 8:1; 45:3; 148:13; Hab. 2:3). This is confirmed by the following statement that He 'shall sit and rule on His throne'. Joshua's coronation was symbolic of that of a worthier One, when the despised Nazarene will be universally acclaimed as King of the kings and Lord of the lords. His rule will not be limited to the tiny state of Israel; Phil. 2:10 indicates that His sovereignty will be acknowledged in the celestial heights, the terrestrial scene and the infernal regions, and Eph. 1:10 reveals that He will be the Divinely-appointed head over the whole creation. Regal glory and the honour and dignity of majesty are to be supremely His.

It was also predicted that He would 'be a priest on His throne'. Barnes maintains that, in view of the next clause, a more appropriate rendering would be, 'there shall be a priest beside His throne', and he identifies the priest as Joshua as the chief counsellor of Zerubbabel, to whom pertained the civil authority. The prophecy looks beyond Joshua and Zerubbabel, however, and we see no reason for departing from the normally accepted view that the reference is to the occupant of the throne, so that Messiah is envisioned as filling the offices of both king and priest. This, of course, was forecast in Ps. 110:4, where Messiah's priesthood was said to be 'after the order of Melchizedek', the priest–king of Gen. 14:18 (see also Heb. 6:20–7:17). Since He would fill both offices, it was added that 'the counsel of peace shall be between them both'. In the past there had not always been complete accord between the priesthood and the monarchy, but all possibility of discord or disagreement was removed if the functions of both were vested in one Person. Messiah would be the securer and dispenser of peace. Moore (op. cit., p. 98) interprets 'the counsel of peace' as 'the counsel that precedes peace, and this is done by Christ in the exercise of these two offices, by one of which He purchases redemption, and by the other applies it; by the one expiates sin, and by the other extirpates it; and thus reconciling man and God, causes peace on earth, and good will to men'.

Perowne's comments are worth quoting. He says (in loc.), 'This has been explained to mean that the two offices, the sacerdotal and the regal, being merged in the one person of Him, who "shall be a priest upon the throne" shall be exercised in perfect harmony, as though a treaty of peace were ratified between them. "The counsel of peace," however, would seem to mean more than this, and to denote a counsel, or measure, devised by "them both", of which the fruit would be peace to those whom it contemplated. This counsel, by which peace is procured and bestowed (Eph. 2:14; John 14:27) is for its execution "between them both", i.e. between the two offices, or rather between the Holder of them both regarded now as King and now as Priest. The view that "them both" refers to the Eternal Father and Messiah, Jehovah and the Branch, though it has been ably advocated, is scarcely warranted by the context, in which the mention of Jehovah is not sufficiently direct and prominent to sustain such a reference.'

The crowns which had been placed upon the head of Joshua were then to be taken and hung in the temple as a memorial – possibly as a reminder of the link between those who had returned from Babylon and those who were still exiled from home. On the basis of Barnes' rendering the crown (or crowns) were for health (or recovery) to Tobijah and Jedaiah and for favour (or beauty) to the son of Zephaniah. The more normal interpretation makes the crown suspended in the temple 'a lasting memorial, not only of the zeal and piety of these offerers of gifts from a far-off land, but also of the kindness shown them by Josiah the son of Zephaniah, who had received them into his house' (cf. Matt. 10:41). If the latter view is taken, the honour paid to the three delegates was surely in their character of representatives of the exiles; the honour paid to their host presumably had reference to more than the hospitality displayed to them, but no other details are given. Some writers find a significance in the materials of which the crown was made, gold being regarded as a type of the deity of Christ, and silver of His redemptive work, but it would be unwise to press the typological significance too far.

The presence of the suspended crown in the temple was also to become a visual intimation, not merely that gifts and offerings would be transmitted by the exiles, but that other contingents would one day return and participate in building the temple of Jehovah – doubtless anticipating the millennial temple. 'The Jews in Judah,' writes Barnes (op. cit., p. 58), 'formed a small, poor and depressed community needing badly the encouragement which could be given by the arrival of co-religionists from afar supplied with means and zealous for the welfare of Jerusalem. Zechariah points to the arrival of the household of Josiah the son of Zephaniah as foreshadowing such reinforcements.' Another *golah*, or new return from Babylon, would assuredly eventuate.

The people's participation in the future blessing was stated to be dependent upon their faithfully rendered obedience to God. The events foretold were in the Divine purpose and would inevitably occur precisely as foretold, but the part they took depended upon themselves. What had occurred, however, was a clear indication that Zechariah (or possibly the angel) had been divinely sent.

CHAPTER 11

Problems of Fasting

There had been a lapse of nearly two years since the events of the first six chapters, without any recorded message through the prophet. Then a deputation arrived at Jerusalem to inquire of the priests and prophets their opinion regarding the necessity for the continuance of a national fast which had been instituted some seven decades before, and the reply to their questions came through the mouth of Zechariah. The circumstances and the problem were detailed in the first three verses of Zech. 7, and the reply was given in four sections, each commencing with the words, 'And the word of Jehovah of hosts came to me, saying . . .' (7:4, 8; 8:1, 18).

'And it came to pass in the fourth year of king Darius that the word of Jehovah came to Zechariah, in the fourth day of the ninth month, Chisleu, when they of Bethel had sent Sherezer and Regem-melech and his men, to entreat the favour of Jehovah and to speak to the priests who were in the house of Jehovah of hosts, and to the prophets, saying, Should I weep in the fifth month, separating myself, as I have done these so many years?' (7:1–3).

The reconstruction of the temple was progressing extremely favourably and in another two years the work would be complete. Although the restoration was not yet finished at the time of this particular incident, the building had reached such a stage that it was evident that the reinstitution of the full services and worship could now be envisaged. It was in these circumstances that a deputation of two men was sent to Jerusalem. The two men concerned were named Sherezer and Regem-melech, and David Baron (op. cit., p. 212) draws attention to the fact that they bore 'foreign names which originally were associated with the false worship of their oppressors. Sharetser was the name of one of the parricide sons of Sennacherib (Isa. 37:38), and also of one of the princes of Babylon who desolated Jerusalem and destroyed the temple (Jer. 39:3–13). The full Assyrian name was Nergal-Sarusur or Nergal-Shar-Ezer, which, according to Schrader, means "May Nergal protect the king". Here

Nergal, the name of the Assyrian false god, is dropped, but the prayer, originally idolatrous, is retained. Regem is found as a proper name in 1 Chron. 2:47. Gesenius explains Regem-melech as signifying "friend of the king". It may originally also have been an Assyrian name.' The two men may have held office in the court of Assyria or Babylonia and to have derived their names from their occupation. Their names may provide a clue to the true reason for their question of the priests and prophets at the city. It is, at any rate, impossible not to be impressed by the contrast between their names and those of the bearers of the gifts referred to in the previous chapter.

According to the A.V., the deputation was sent to the house of God or Bethel (which is literally 'house of God'). But the temple was never described in this fashion and there seems little doubt that the wording should read, 'when they of Bethel had sent'. Bethel was one of the cities to which some of the exiles had returned (Ezra. 2:28; Neh. 11:31). It lay to the north of Jerusalem and had been a religious centre in the kingdom of Israel until the latter's fall. It was here that Jeroboam set up the golden calves and it had been a centre for idolatrous worship (1 Kings 12:28; 13:1; Amos 7:13). The fact that the people of Bethel now sent to Jerusalem was a clear indication that they did not anticipate the revival of the ten-tribed kingdom of Israel and that they recognized the kingdom of Judah as the only national hope. As another says, 'Notwithstanding the many sacred memories connected with their city, and the fact that it had been the seat of a temple in the days of the Israelitish kingdom, to which the tribes of Israel had resorted in numbers, no attempt was now made on their part to dispute the legitimate right of Jerusalem being regarded as the only place where the sacrifices and services enjoined by the precepts of the Mosaic law could be offered.'

The Bethel representatives came to Jerusalem to entreat the Divine favour and to consult the priests in the temple and also the prophets (presumably Zechariah and Haggai). Seventy years earlier Nebuchadnezzar had destroyed the temple of Solomon and most of the buildings of Jerusalem by fire. This had occurred in the fifth month (August) of the year, and from the seventh to the tenth day of the month, the flames had raged through the doomed city (2 Kings 25:8, 9; Jer. 52:13). The

Jews had instituted a special fast in commemoration of the event, and they had observed it as a period of mourning for seventy years. They had fasted and wept, had worn sackcloth and had rent their clothes in memory of the national calamity. It was not a divinely ordained fast and had not been required of God. At the same time, if it was a season of true humiliation and penitence, the observance would have had a spiritual significance and value. Fasting *per se* was not meritorious, but it could have the effect of teaching the mourner his utter dependence upon God. But it was clear that this particular fast had become symptomatic of the mechanical formalism and religious externalism of a people who were weary of what had become a meaningless ritualism. In any case, now that the temple was being rebuilt, this fast seemed completely pointless and superfluous. Surely it was a work of supererogation, significant while the temple lay waste, but meaningless now that it was being restored. It was in this spirit that the messengers came to Jerusalem.

They posed their question to priests and prophets. Was it necessary in present circumstances, to abstain from normal practices and to devote themselves to lamenting the destruction of a temple which was now being rebuilt? There is an indication that they were, in fact, weary of the practice and all that it entailed, for the messengers referred to the people having abstained from meat and drink (or 'separating' themselves) 'these so many years'. The fast had become a legalistic ritual in which they had no heart. Chambers (in loc.) says that fasting 'is an expression of sorrow and humiliation proper to be used on the occasions which call for great feelings; then it is fitted to help the discipline of the soul and to lead to benefits quite beyond itself. . . . But whenever the exercise is made to recur statedly at regular intervals without regard to circumstances, its inevitable tendency is to degenerate into a barren form and a mischievous self-deception.' This is what had happened to them. The fast, instituted by their fathers (doubtless well-intended and commendable, even though not divinely appointed) had become devoid of spiritual import or value. It irked them and they wanted to put an end to it. Their current conditions might have been construed as a call to what one writer terms 'continued fasting and humiliation', but they were oblivious to their spiritual need.

The Divine reply to the question which so agitated them was, as already indicated, given in four sections, viz. 7:4–7; 7:8–14; 8:1–17; and 8:18–23. The parenthesis in 8:1–17 is not, of course, irrelevant to the reply, but did not, in itself, really constitute part of the direct answer. The first section of the reply was couched in the form of a reproof.

'Then came the word of Jehovah of hosts to me, saying, Speak to all the people of the land, and to the priests, saying, When you fasted and mourned in the fifth and seventh month, even those seventy years, did you at all fast to me, even to me? And when you eat and drink, is it not you who eat and drink? Should you not hear the words which Jehovah cried by the former prophets, when Jerusalem was inhabited and in prosperity, and the cities thereof round about her, when men inhabited the south and the plain?' (7:4–7).

God's answer was not given directly to the two delegates from Bethel. Zechariah was commanded to address his words to all the people of the land, including the priests. (No mention is made of the prophets, from which it may presumably be deduced that the prophets referred to in verse 3 were merely Zechariah and Haggai). The question had been propounded to the priests, but they had evidently been incapable of providing the counsel sought, and since God's message was addressed *inter alia* to them, the inference is that they were as culpable as the rest of the nation of substituting external formalism for inward reality. It is a salutary thought that even the leaders of God's people can lose sight of spiritual realities and see nothing more than forms and ceremonies – a lifeless ritual bringing no honour to God or blessing to man.

The reply referred not only to the fast in the fifth month, which had been the subject of the inquiry, but also to the fast in the seventh month. It was in that month that Gedaliah, the governor appointed by Nebuchadnezzar, had been murdered by Ishmael and his supporters and that the rest of the people left in the land of Judah fled to Egypt for fear of the murder being avenged upon them by the Chaldeans (2 Kings 25:25, 26). This completed the calamities of Judah and was virtually the end of the little state for the time being and, in memory of this further trouble they had instituted another day of mourning and fasting. Neh. 9:1 refers to another fast (probably a special one and not an annual event) on the twenty-fourth day of the seventh month on which the people confessed their sins in sackcloth and ashes. The day of atonement was also celebrated on the tenth day of the same month (Lev. 16:29). It is reasonably clear however, that the reply related only to the two fasts which the Jews had instituted and made no reference to Nehemiah's fast or to the day of atonement (Lev. 23:26–32).

The seventy years' servitude to Babylon (Jer. 25:11) would expire at the next fast, and the people were challenged by the One who realized that the question they had posed was symptomatic of their real attitude to Him. When they had fasted during those seventy years, He asked, had they sincerely fasted to Him? Were they not more concerned with their loss of home and material possessions, with the indignity they had suffered of exile from their own land, and with the humiliation of servitude to a pagan country? Their abstinence from food, their mourning and lamentation had not been an expression of contrition for their transgressions, or a recognition of the justice of the Divine hand which had inflicted chastisement upon them. Their legalistic asceticism and their punctilious observance of their self-appointed fasts were little more than an indication of their grief for their own distress and personal loss. It was concerned with self and not with God, and He virtually exposed their insincerity and self-centredness. He was more interested in truth than in sackcloth.

If their fasting sprang from selfish motives, their feasting was no more commendable. It was equally as egoistic and, by implication, just as God-dishonouring. Their concern was only to satisfy their natural appetite, and they paid no regard to the One by whom even the material benefits of life are bestowed, and they clearly gave no thought to the needs of others who were less fortunate than themselves. Their actions were a barometer, revealing their spiritual attitude and condition. The reference was not merely, of course, to the appointed feasts (Lev. 23), but to the basic practice in connection with the Levitical offerings, where, except in the case of burnt offerings (which were devoted entirely to God), the worshipper and his family feasted upon part of the offering after the appointed portion had been presented to God and the priest's portion had been given to him (cf. Deut. 12:5–7) There seemed no appreciation of the relationship of the eating and drinking to the sacrifice which had just previously been offered, and no understanding of the spiritual significance of the actions.

Zechariah reminded the people of the messages proclaimed by earlier prophets in the days of peace and tranquillity, when Jerusalem and the other cities were safe and prosperous, fully populated centres, when the southern Negev was fertile and inhabited, and the Shephelah, or lowland country, experienced the blessings of nature. Judah was divided into (1) the Negev or south, (2) the Shephelah, the stretch of low hills running from north to south, and (3) the hill country (i.e. Jerusalem and the cities referred to). The remonstrances made by God in those earlier days went unheeded, but they were still relevant: ought not Judah to listen to them now? Their fathers had refused to respond to the prophets' pleas for repentance and had ignored their warnings of consequent judgement. There was a danger that the returned exiles might be just as obtuse and would lapse into the same ways. By inference, the blessings enjoyed in pre-exile days could be restored if the people turned in sincerity of heart to Jehovah; the prophet's words were still pertinent, and neglect of God's claims could only result once again in Divine discipline. This was, in fact, what actually occurred. Even today, we avoid the message at our own peril.

The second section of the reply dealt with the cause of the chastisement inflicted upon people and land.

'And the word of Jehovah came to Zechariah, saying, Thus speaks Jehovah of hosts, saying, Render a judicial decision based on truth, and show kindness and compassion every man to his brother, and oppress not the widow, nor the fatherless, the sojourner nor the poor; and let none of you devise evil against his brother in your heart. But they refused to hear, and gave a rebellious shoulder, and made heavy their ears, that they might not hear. Yes, they made their hearts as an adamant stone, lest they should hear the law, and the words which Jehovah of hosts has sent by his Spirit by the former prophets. Therefore came great wrath from Jehovah of hosts. Therefore it is come to pass that, just as He cried and they would not hear: so they shall cry and I will not hear, says Jehovah of hosts: but I will scatter them with a whirlwind among all the nations whom they have not known. Thus the land was desolate after them, so that no man passed through nor returned: for they laid the pleasant land desolate' (7:8–14).

In the second section of the reply to the Bethel delegates, the prophecy emphasized by implication the conduct which had eventuated in the judgement experienced by the earlier generation. Barnes says (op. cit., pp. 61, 62), 'The prophet never forgets the awful chastisement inflicted on his people for their past sins of oppression, and by reminding them of it, he warns them against persisting in similar sins in the present. The Jewish nobles were themselves in a depressed condition, and yet they in turn became oppressors of their weaker brethren.' Zechariah accordingly again explained the necessity for moral and spiritual reformation in substitution for the external observances which had been the subject of the Bethelites' inquiry. The reality of their attitude to God was evidenced by their attitude to their fellow-men and the prophet reiterated the age-long principles which should govern the relationship of man with man. Those principles were to be seen in God's dealings with His creatures, and He expected His people to follow the pattern thus set.

To others, to whom fasting was proving irksome in their day, a message had been given through Isaiah at an earlier date, 'Is not this the fast that I have chosen? to loose the bands of wickedness, to undo the heavy burdens, and to let the oppressed go free, and that you break every yoke? Is it not to deal your bread to the hungry, and that you bring the poor who are afflicted to your house? When you see the naked to cover him; and that you hide not yourself from your own flesh?' (Isa. 58:6, 7). There should be true judgement or perfect justice, and mercy and kindness should be practised to others. In pity and compassion, they should refrain from oppressing the widow and orphan, the stranger and the poor. These were specific injunctions under the Mosaic law (Exod. 22:21, 22; see also Isa. 1:17). Fraud and violence were the evidence of a heart turned away from God. The devising of evil against others was not to be allowed in their thoughts.

Yet it was just in these respects that their fathers had failed (Isa. 10:1, 2; Jer. 5:28). They had refused to listen to the Divine injunctions and, like an ox intractably refusing to be yoked, they had obdurately resisted the imposition of any control or restraint by God. In their recusance they had closed their ears to the Divine admonitions and pleas, and had resolutely hardened their hearts. They were adamant in their refusal to listen to the commands of the *Torah*, reiterated as they had been in the messages sent by the prophets of an earlier day.

Since that earlier generation would listen to neither the law nor the prophets, Divine wrath fell upon them. So serious was their refractory disobedience that the judgement meted out to them was a punitive and unmitigated infliction. They had suffered under the hand of the Chaldeans, but the latter were simply the instrument of God. Moore says (op. cit., p. 109), 'As they refused to wear the yoke of obedience, God laid upon them the yoke of oppression; and as they hardened their hearts like the diamond against God's words, God broke these hard hearts by His judgements.' But their descendants continued blindly and impenitently, refusing to conceive that the same judgement might fall upon them.

Jeremiah had warned their fathers that Jehovah would bring evil upon them which they would be unable to escape and God had declared, 'though they shall cry to Me, I will not hearken to them' (Jer. 11:11). What he had foretold had come to pass. When God had cried to the people, they had refused to listen. When later they realized their jeopardy, they cried to Him in their extremity, but then He refused to listen. The experience of the past should have been a warning to the present generation.

Because of the impenitence of their fathers, judgement had fallen, and God had whirled them away like a mighty hurricane (cf. Job. 27:21; Amos 1:14), scattering them among nations who were strangers to them. Their land was laid waste and no one passed through or returned. It had been a pleasant or desirable land, but the nations had made it desolate. The experience was so recent in history that it should have needed no emphasis, but should have been effective in winning back to God the descendants of those who had suffered the Divine discipline, but it seemed to have made little more than a temporary impression. Man never seems to learn the lessons of history and what was true of Judah is equally true of God's people today.

CHAPTER 12

Restoration to Blessing

'Jerusalem in the prophet's day was still for the most part in ruins and grievously depopulated,' wrote Barnes (op. cit., p. 64). 'Nothing except the "zeal of Jehovah" could restore it to any measure of its former prosperity. But Zechariah is assured that if his people repent, Jehovah will indeed be zealous in their behalf. So he promises that exiles shall return from east and west to replenish Jerusalem, and the city shall be at peace and in security again and filled with rejoicing.' The next section of the reply to the Bethel delegation, therefore, anticipated the future blessing and prosperity in the millennial age, and regarded the partial restoration of Zechariah's day as the symbol and precursor of what was yet to happen. The eighth chapter was divided into ten subsections, each marked by the introductory phrase, 'Thus says Jehovah' (vv. 2, 3, 4, 6, 7, 9, 14, 19, 20, 23).

'Again the word of Jehovah of hosts came, saying, Thus says Jehovah of hosts, I am jealous for Zion with great jealousy, and I am jealous for her with great wrath. Thus says Jehovah, I am returned to Zion, and will dwell in the midst of Jerusalem: and Jerusalem shall be called the city of truth; and the mountain of Jehovah of hosts, the holy mountain. Thus says Jehovah of hosts, There shall yet old men and old women dwell in the streets of Jerusalem, and every man with his staff in his hands for very age. And the streets of the city shall be full of boys and girls playing in the streets. Thus says Jehovah of hosts. If it be marvellous in the eyes of the remnant of this people in those days, should it also be marvellous in my eyes? says Jehovah of hosts. Thus says Jehovah of hosts, Behold, I will bring them and they shall dwell in the midst of Jerusalem: and they shall be my people and I will be their God in truth and righteousness. Thus says Jehovah of hosts, Let your hands be strong, you that hear in these days these words from the mouth of the prophets, which were spoken concerning the day that the foundation of the house of Jehovah of hosts was laid, even the temple, that it might be built.

For before those days there was no return for his labour for man nor any for beast; neither was there any peace to him that went out or come in because of the adversary: for I set all men every one against his neighbour. But now I will not be to the remnant of this people as in the former days, says Jehovah of hosts. For the seed of peace, the vine, shall give its fruits, and the ground shall give its increase, and the heavens shall give their dew; and I will cause the remnant of this people to inherit all these things. And it shall come to pass that, as you were a curse among the heathen, O house of Judah and house of Israel, so will I now save you and you shall be a blessing. Fear not, but let your hands be strong. For thus says Jehovah of hosts, As I thought to punish you, when your fathers provoked me to wrath, says Jehovah of hosts, and I repented not; so again have I thought in these days to do good to Jerusalem and to the house of Judah. Fear you not. These are the things that you shall do. Speak every man the truth to his neighbour; execute the judgement of truth and peace in your gates; and let none of you devise evil in your hearts against his neighbour; and love no false oath: for all these are things that I hate, says Jehovah' (8:1–17).

Zech. 8 was still part of the reply to the Bethelite inquiry regarding fasting, although the answer was virtually not given until the second section of the chapter. The first section (vv. 1–17) was composed of a series of promises to Judah of future blessing, each introduced – as already mentioned – by the phrase, 'Thus says Jehovah'. This first section portrayed the restoration of peace, happiness and prosperity to Jerusalem and the people of Judah, and indicated the intense interest still displayed by Jehovah in this wayward nation. Despite all their failures His affection was still set upon them and He declared that He was jealous for Zion with great jealousy and great fury.

Because of the nation's sin, unrelieved judgement fell upon them. God left them to their foes and allowed them to be carried away captive and their country to be depopulated and devastated. The vehemence of His anger and the severity of their punishment had been justified in view of their disloyalty and idolatry. But now God had resumed His relationship with His people and had returned to Zion. (This statement was not completely applicable in Zechariah's day and was patently predictive of a day which is yet to come.) His people's former distress was, however, to be banished by the realization of His presence in the midst of them, for He would actually dwell in Jerusalem. By implication, the temple would be completed and He would take up His residence as in the days of old. It seems evident that the promise extends beyond Zerubbabel's temple and the immediate circumstances of Judah to a period still future, when the glory of God will again be seen in a millennial temple and His presence will be realized in blessing in Jerusalem (Ezek. 43:2–7; 44:4).

By His sanctifying presence, the city of Jerusalem, which had proved so unfaithful and disloyal to Him, would become the city of truth and holiness. Isaiah had described the city as a harlot and the abode of murderers, but even he had foreseen the day when Jerusalem would be renamed 'the city of righteousness, the faithful city' (Isa 1:21, 26). Although this may have been partially fulfilled in the days of Zerubbabel, Zech. 14:20, 21 makes it evident that the prophecy was looking on to the still future period of millennial blessing. Even the mountain of Jehovah, 'which had been a heap of ruins, shall again be the holy mountain, where the Holy One will sit in the majesty of His unchanging justice and mercy' (Smith).

Jerusalem had suffered the ravages of war; her buildings had been torn down; her inhabitants had been either massacred or deported; disease had swept over the tragic metropolis. The old people had been killed, and any young ones who survived had been carried away as captives. All that was now to end. The city was to be restored to its former condition, and death should no longer stalk its streets. Once the parks and thoroughfares had been filled with soldiers' camps: now they were to be filled with old and young, enjoying the city's newfound peace and tranquillity. The aged, supported by their sticks, would walk without fear in the streets, and the city would resound with the mirth and merry laughter of the happy carefree children playing in the streets (cf. Matt. 11:16). In the times of the Maccabees, we are told that 'the ancient men sat all in the streets, communing together of good things' (1 Macc. 14:19) and, in a coming day, the conditions will, of course, be seen once again. This might now seem marvellous to the remnant of the people. The transformation predicted must have appeared almost incredible, but God declared that it would not be marvellous in His eyes.

The things that are impossible with man are possible with God.

In 721 B.C. the ten tribes of Israel had been deported to Assyria, and in 598 and 589 B.C. the majority of Judah had been removed as captives to Babylon and, although some returned to their own land under Joshua and Zerubbabel, the majority presumably did not. With the destruction of Jerusalem by the Romans in A.D. 70 and the quashing of the rebellion of Bar Cochba in A.D. 134 the Jews were not normally allowed access to Jerusalem. They were dispersed all over the world, but principally in countries to the west of their own country. God now declared that He would regather His people from the east and the west and bring them home to dwell in Jerusalem. (Jerusalem doubtless was a metonymy for the country as a whole.) This, of course, has never yet been completely fulfilled, but Isaiah declares that, in the day of Messiah's presence, 'Jehovah shall set his hand again the second time to recover the remnant of His people, who shall be left . . . and gather together the dispersed of Judah from the four corners of the earth' (Isa. 11:11, 12, and reiterates the Divine promise, 'I will bring your seed from the east, and gather you from the west; I will say to the north, Give up; and to the south, Keep not back: bring my sons from far, and my daughters from the ends of the earth' (Isa. 43:5, 6). Although Jews have returned to their own land, the universal regathering predicted by the prophet has patently not yet taken place, and the national acknowledgement of God which he foresaw has certainly not yet occurred.

Jehovah declared that He would bring the exiles to dwell in the midst of Jerusalem. In that day they will be His people and He will be their God in truth and righteousness. There has hitherto been no spiritual regeneration of the nation of the character implied by the prophet, and it is, therefore, clear that the restoration referred to is that which is to occur after our Lord's return to earth. It is then that Jehovah will become their God in truth and righteousness, i.e. to quote another, 'Jehovah will be true to His people and perhaps perform acts of righteousness for them, and conversely His people will be true to Him, and will act righteously one to another.'

Although these promises will not find their consummation until the millennial age, they would, of course, have come into effect immediately had the Jews of our Lord's day accepted Him.

Their rejection of Him has postponed the fulfilment of these prophecies of future blessing. The people were, however, exhorted to strengthen their hands, in view of the words uttered by the prophets when the foundation of the temple was laid seventeen years before. Although the reference is primarily to exhortations of Haggai and Zechariah (see Ezra 5:1, 2) at that time, there is doubtless also the inference that the promises just uttered should be a further incentive to unflagging effort in the rebuilding of the temple.

Haggai tells the story of the trials experienced by the people. They had been forbidden to continue the work (Ezra 4:21) and they had supinely accepted the royal prohibition. But their failure had met with Divine chastisement. Crops had failed and trade had dwindled to negligible proportions. A severe economic depression had led to unemployment and to poor recompense even when there was work (Hag. 1:6). Men and animals were both affected. Internecine strife and dissension had resulted and the spirit of true neighbourliness had evaporated. The nation's sufferings had been the discipline of God for their neglect of His work and their virtual apostasy from Him. But His attitude to the remnant of His people was about to change.

The vine (frequently used as a type of Israel), described as the seed of peace because it can flourish only when conditions are peaceful and the land is not suffering the ravages of war, would now prove fruitful. (Most commentators interpret verse 12 as 'There shall be a sowing of seed in peace' and take the reference to the vine as a separate clause.) The ground would no longer be sterile, but would yield her crops. The heavens had given no dew (Hag. 1:10), but they would now supply the constant need of moisture. And all these would be the heritage of the remnant in the land.

Addressing both Israel and Judah, not only in anticipation of the future, but also because there had been representatives of both among the exiles who had returned from Babylon, God declared that they had been an object of cursing, scattered among the nations (Jer. 24:9). Unger (op. cit., p. 143) says that the 'curse was predicted as the result of apostasy and sin (Deut. 28:15–62) and was to eventuate in the punishment of a worldwide dispersion (Deut. 28:63–68). The full reach of Zechariah's words extends to the sufferings and persecutions of this final diaspora, sweeping the entire span of the *loammi* period when their national election has been set aside (Rom. 11:1–12).' Just as they had been a curse, however, Jehovah would now save them and they would be an object of blessing. Therefore, they should strengthen their hands and busy themselves in the building of the temple. When their fathers had provoked God to wrath by their transgressions, it had been His mind to punish the nation and he did not relent in pouring out His anger. So it was now His purpose to do well to Jerusalem and Judah. They were not to fear.

God then set out the principles which should guide His people's lives. Jerusalem was to become the city of truth and holiness (v. 3). Consequently truth should characterize personal intercourse between its inhabitants (cf. Zeph. 3:13), and truth and peace the administration of justice in the city. (The 'gates' of verse 16 were the place at which cases were judged and the administration of the city took place). He had previously told the Bethelite deputation not to devise evil in their hearts against their brother (7:10), and the same injunction was reiterated that none in Judah should devise evil in their hearts against their neighbours. Perjury was a common sin of the period: the people were now commanded to love no false oath – a stronger expression than to swear none – since untruth was detestable to God. He sought sincerity and reality.

The same principles are, of course, applicable to the Christian today. The one who follows Christ will be characterized by righteousness and practical holiness, by truth and fairness and his relations with his fellow-men will display his honesty of purpose and freedom from evil intent.

The last six verses of the chapter formed the fourth and final section of the reply to the Bethelites and showed the complete transformation which was to take place in a future day.

'And the word of Jehovah of hosts came to me, saying, Thus says Jehovah of hosts, The fast of the fourth month, and the fast of the fifth and the fast of the seventh, and the fast of the tenth, shall be to the house of Judah joy and gladness, and cheerful feasts; therefore love truth and peace. Thus says Jehovah of hosts, It shall yet come to pass that there will come peoples and the inhabitants of many cities. And the inhabitants of one city will go to another, saying, Let us go speedily to entreat the favour of Jehovah and to seek Jehovah of hosts. I will go also. Yes, many peoples and strong nations will come to seek Jehovah of hosts in Jerusalem, and to entreat the favour of Jehovah. Thus says Jehovah of hosts, In those days it shall come to pass that ten men out of all languages of the nations will take hold, will even take hold of the skirt of him that is a Jew, saying, We will go with you, for we have heard that God is 'with you' (8:18–23).

In the concluding section of this part of the book, the question posed by the deputation from Bethel was answered in a manner that must have been totally unexpected. They had inquired about the necessity for the continued observance of the fast in the fifth month which their predecessors had instituted (7:3). The reply referred to four fasts: the first, in the fourth month, instituted as a reminder of the capture of Jerusalem by Nebuchadnezzar (Jer. 39:2); the second, in the fifth month, which commemorated the burning to the ground of the city of Jerusalem and of the temple (2 Kings 25:8); the third, in the seventh month, which commemorated Gedaliah's murder (Jer. 41:2); and the fourth, in the tenth month, which related to the commencement of the siege of Jerusalem (2 Kings 25:1). All of these fasts had been instituted by the people themselves and without any Divine direction to do so. The divinely appointed fast of the Day of Atonement on the tenth day of the seventh month (Lev. 16) was evidently not under review. The exiles had consistently observed the four fasts mentioned with sorrowful hearts, albeit, as God had previously indicated, with no real grief for their sins nor contrition towards Him. But now these periods of mourning were going to be transformed into seasons of joy and gladness (cf. Isa. 61:2, 3). They were to become no longer fasts but cheerful feasts. It is clear that this has not yet become true in Israel's history and that one must look on to the millennium for the complete fulfilment of the Divine promises. In view of the coming substitution of joy for sorrow and happiness for mourning, the command was repeated that the people were to love truth and peace.

From the cities of Israel and Judah (the former must presumably have been implied if the message was to be of any comfort to the Bethelites) the people (i.e. the tribes of Israel, as in Deut. 33:3, 19, and not the foreign nations referred to in verse 22) will come in that day, joining together to seek God's face at Jerusalem, and persuading others to join them. So complete will be the turning to God that some straggler, realizing the urge, will say, 'I will go also'. (The implication may possibly, however, be that, when the inhabitants of one city eagerly run to beseech other cities to go, the instant reply is an indication of readiness to go too.) 'Thus they start, not by ones and twos, but in crowds to hasten to Jerusalem, that they may secure the favour of God.'

The enthusiasm will spread to other nations and Gentile peoples will also make their way up to the city (Mic. 4:2) to seek the favour of Jehovah. As they draw near to the holy city, the Gentiles surround any Jew in sight, ten (i.e. metaphorically, a large number) of them seizing the edge of his shawl or outer garment to identify themselves with him, will declare their intention of going with him, because they have heard that God (Elohim) is with him. 'When this prediction was uttered,' writes Moore (op. cit., p. 123), 'nothing seemed more hopelessly improbable than its fulfilment. The Jews were a poor, despised, obscure tribe in the heart of Syria, whose existence was only known to the mighty world by their furnishing a trophy to the victorious arms of Babylon. Greece was just rising in the firmament of human history, and as she ascended to her brilliant zenith, her track was marked by the sweeping of the phalanxes of Alexander and the legions of Antiochus over the hills and valleys of Judea. And yet this prophecy remained unfulfilled. Rome was then in the rugged feebleness of her wolf-nursed infancy, and slowly continued to grow until she reached that gigantic stature in which she ruled the earth, and her conquering legions under Pompey again swept over the fated land.' The centuries have passed and other empires have filled the world's stage and have disappeared from view. But one day, what seems so improbable now will be a realized fact, and Jerusalem, the city of the great King, will be the centre of the earth.

CHAPTER 13

The Conquests of Alexander

Chapters 9 to 14 form the second part of the book of Zechariah and it is probable that several years had elapsed since the first part had been uttered. The building of the temple had been completed and the levitical forms of worship had been reinstated. The six chapters look on to the first and second advents of the Messiah and are divided into two sections (Chapters 9 to 11, and 12 to 14), each described as a 'burden of the word of Jehovah'. The 'burden' may mean the utterance of God or the pronounced judgement of God, and it has been interpreted as a burdensome message. 'It is an oracle that is heavy, freighted with war or judgement' says one writer.

The fact that the prophet's name is not mentioned in the whole of these chapters and that the style is so different from that of the first eight chapters of the book has led to doubts regarding the Zecharian authorship, although the canonicity of the chapters does not seem ever to have been questioned. The primary reason adduced for the doubt is not, however, the absence of the prophet's name or the difference in style, but the New Testament ascription (in Matt. 27:9, 10) of the authorship of Zech. 11:12, 13 to Jeremiah and not to Zechariah. Fuller reference is made to this later and it may suffice, for the time being, to point out that the passage in question was ascribed to Zechariah in the days of our Lord and the New Testament writers for it occupied the same place in the Septuagint, which was completed three centuries earlier, and which was used by our Lord and the apostles. One writer pertinently remarks, 'It does not seem probable that the Evangelist would make a correction of the Jewish canon in this indirect manner, without giving some intimation to that effect'. Taking all the facts into consideration, there seems no substantial reason for questioning the date or authority of these chapters.

Through the centuries, both Israel and Judah had suffered from the active opposition of their neighbours, but now these were to be dealt with for their oppression and enmity, and

Zechariah disclosed the manner in which their retribution would come. Even if the date of this second part of the book was towards the end of the prophet's life, the events foretold still lay in the future, and the empire which God purposed to use as His instrument for the castigation of His people's foes had not yet come into existence. With meticulous accuracy, however, Zechariah described the military activities and conquests of the Macedonian empire, particularly as they related to God's people and to their land. The details recorded are, in fact, so remarkably accurate that they constitute one of the strongest evidences of the reliability and inspiration of the book.

The first 'burden' concerned Syria, Phoenicia, and Philistia.

'The burden of the word of Jehovah upon the land of Hadrach, and Damascus shall be its resting-place: for the eyes of man, as of all the tribes of Israel, shall be toward Jehovah. And Hamath also which borders thereon; Tyre and Zidon, because she is very wise. And Tyre did build herself a stronghold, and heaped up silver as the dust, and fine gold as the mire of the streets. Behold, the Lord will dispossess her and he will smite her power in the sea; and she shall be consumed by fire. Ashkelon shall see it and fear; Gaza also shall see it and tremble exceedingly; and Ekron for her expectation shall be put to shame. And the king shall perish from Gaza, and Ashkelon shall not be inhabited. And a mongrel race shall dwell in Ashdod, and I will cut off the pride of the Philistines, and I will remove his blood out of his mouth, and his abominations from between his teeth: but he also shall remain as a remnant for our God, and he shall be as a chieftian in Judah, and Ekron as a Jebusite. And I will encamp about my house against the army, that none pass through or return: and no oppressor shall pass through them any more: for now have I seen with my eyes' (9:1–8).

'The eyes of all look unto thee,' declared the psalmist (Ps. 145:12). 'Our eyes are upon thee,' said Jehoshaphat in the day of Judah's extremity (2 Chron. 20:12). Zechariah declared that the burden was pronounced because the eyes of man, as of all the tribe of Israel, were towards the Lord, but the significance may possibly be that Jehovah's eyes were upon man and upon all the tribes of Israel. C. H. H. Wright, however, considers that the import is that, 'When the fulfilment of the oracles takes place upon Hadrach and Damascus, and the wrath of God descends upon those cities and districts, the eyes of the nations as well as those of the people of Israel will look towards Jehovah, and marvel at the wonders of judgement which will then be performed in their sight in accordance with the solemn warnings of the prophet.' This is perhaps the most logical interpretation. The prophecy indicated that judgement was to fall upon Hadrach, Damascus and Hamath of Syria, Tyre and Sidon of Phoenicia, and Ashkelon, Gaza, Ebron and Ashdod of Philistia.

Some doubt exists regarding the identity of Hadrach, but Sir H. Rawlinson said some years ago, 'It is now certain that there was a city called Hadrach in the neighbourhood of Damascus and Hamath, although the exact site is unknown.' But Laetsch (op. cit., p. 450) says, 'Hadrach, for centuries a puzzling historical problem, has now been definitely identified with Hatarika mentioned in the annals of Assyrian kings as an Aramaean country near Damascus and Hamath, against which Assyria campaigned in 772, 755 and 733 B.C.' The three cities of Hadrach, Damascus and Hamath together represented Syria and they shared the same fate at the hands of the conqueror.

While the judgement was to fall upon Syria, as represented by three of its principal cities it was to remain upon Damascus (cf. Zech. 6:8). The punitive hand of Jehovah was to fall upon the city, not to destroy it or to put an end to its existence, for it still continues to the present day. Judgement was to light upon Damascus and settle there: retribution would justly fall upon the oppressor and particularly upon the city, primarily responsible. For centuries Damascus had been the formidable and bitter foe of God's people, but she was now to suffer herself. Hamath, bordering on Damascus, would also share similarly the punishment to be meted out by God.

The period described by the prophecy is undoubtedly that of Alexander the Great in the fourth century B.C. Alexander was one of the most remarkable administrators and military leaders in history. Succeeding his father Philip, as King of Macedon at the youthful age of 20 in 336 B.C., he brought a great part of the world under his control. H. A. L. Fisher, in *A History of Europe* (p. 42), says that in his short reign of thirteen years, he 'reasserted the Macedonian authority in Hellas and Thrace, levelled

Thebes to the ground, conquered with his small, mobile and most effective army, Asia Minor, Syria, Egypt, and Persia, and marched his Macedonian veterans over the Khyber Pass into the plains of India'. When Alexander invaded Asia Minor he first defeated the Persian army at the passage of the river Granicus and then took most of Asia Minor before routing the forces of Darius near the city of Issus in 333 B.C. He swept on to subdue Syria and Phoenicia, the city of Tyre being finally subjugated in 332 B.C., before an expedition was made against Egypt and Libya and then against Babylon. The young king was undoubtedly the instrument of God and his conquests fulfilled several of the Old Testament prophecies.

Zechariah disclosed how the punishment of the oppressors of Judah and Israel would occur. Following the battle of Issus, Alexander set out to conquer Syria. He sent Parmenio to capture Damascus, at which Darius had deposited a large amount of treasure, and to take possession of the Persian's wealth. One after another, practically all of the Syrian cities capitulated without offering any resistance. According to the prophet, Tyre and Sidon were to be the next to fall a prey to the conqueror. Sidon did, in fact, quickly surrender, but Tyre considered herself completely impregnable and she refused entry to the Macedonian. Tyre was commonly termed the queen of the sea and she claimed to have invented and taught the principles of navigation. Her position seemed secure, but she had invoked judgement. M. Rollin says in *Ancient History* (volume II p. 87). 'She was not satisfied with having reduced the Jews to a state of captivity, notwithstanding the alliance between them; with selling them to the Gentiles, and delivering them up to their most cruel enemies (Joel 3:4–8; Amos 1:9, 10): she likewise had seized upon the inheritance of the Lord, and carried away from His temple the most precious things to enrich therewith the temples of her idols.' Their actions attracted God's vengeance (Ezek. 26:3–12, 19; 27:27, 34), but it was not until Alexander's day that the predicted punishment really fell (Isa. 23:1–9). Tyre boasted of her wisdom, but it was ineffective to deliver her.

Zechariah declared that she had built herself a stronghold and had heaped up silver as dust and gold as mire in the streets. Although she was one of the richest and most prosperous commercial cities in the world, the reference to the city's wealth was presumably intended as a contemptuous assessment of it as worthless in practice. In dry weather the dust was a nuisance to the citizens, but the inspired word describes Tyre's silver as a heap of dust, which would, of course, be scattered in the wind. In the wet weather the mud or mire would be an equal nuisance in the unpaved streets, but this was the simile used for the Tyrians' store of gold. Ezek. 28, which, like Zech. 9, referred to the wisdom of Tyre, also referred to her opulence and deliberate amassing of gold and silver and implied that this was one of the causes of her downfall. She was the emporium of the world's most varied and rare products: gold and precious stones from Ethiopia and Arabia, silver from Spain, emeralds from Damascus, wheat, honey and oil from Palestine, linen from Egypt, ivory from the East. She carried most of the world's trade by ship.

Zechariah's statement that she had built herself a stronghold is a paronomasia in Hebrew – *Tsur* (Tyre) and *Matsor* (stronghold). Old Tyre on the mainland was destroyed by Nebuchadnezzar, 240 years before Alexander. At the time to which the prophecy related, the city was no longer situated, even partly, on the mainland, but on an island about half a mile from the shore. It was nearly twenty miles in circumference and was surrounded by massive walls 150 feet high. 'Proudly confident in the strength of their island fortress,' says C. H. H. Wright, 'the Tyrians mocked the attempts of Alexander to reduce their city. Every engine of war suited for defence had been stored up in their bulwarks, and every device which their skilful engineers could suggest was had recourse to and for a time with marked success.' It was obvious that the only way in which the city could be attacked was by building a causeway from the mainland to the island, and Alexander stripped Old Tyre of stones and rubbish for this purpose, thus fulfilling Ezek. 26:4–12. His mole was demolished by the defenders and ravaged by storm, but he patiently went on building and ultimately it was completed. The mole, in fact, was so well built and so great in size that it has permanently converted Tyre from an island into a promontory. With Cyprian and Phoenician fleets blockading the harbour, the Macedonian forces attacked and captured the fortified city, massacred 10,000 of its defenders and sold the rest into slavery. Tyre had withstood a five years' siege by the Assyrians and a thirteen years' siege by the Chaldeans, but Alexander took it after a siege of seven months. God had foretold that it would become a bare rock and a place for the spreading of nets (Ezek. 26:14). Keith says that on his visit there, he 'came suddenly on five or six fishermen sitting on some prostrate columns, with their nets spread on the sand upon the site of the mole "in the midst of the sea."'.

Tyre was (*a*) to be dispossessed, (*b*) to have her power smitten in the sea, and (*c*) to be consumed by fire. Patently she was literally ejected and dispossessed by the victorious Macedonians. Regarding the second point Pusey says, 'The scene of her pride was to be that of her overthrow; the waves which girt her round should bury her ruins and wash over her site. Even in the sea the hand of God should find her and smite her in it and into it, and so that she should abide in it.' Thirdly, the city was actually consumed by fire when all of its inhabitants had been put to death. God's threatened judgements have been executed. As one writer says, 'Over 200 years before Nebuchadnezzar's siege Joel foretold her judgement; then Isaiah in 712 B.C., Ezekiel in 590, and Zechariah in 457. Yet still judgement lingered. Again and again Tyre was overthrown, but not obliterated. In the days of Jerome, in the fifth century, it was an opulent city. In the time of the Crusades it was still a city. But in 1291 the Mohammedan approached. In terror the Tyrians took to their ships in mass, never to return. The Sultan of Egypt overthrew the city, choked her matchless harbour with her ruins, cast into the sea statues and columns, and the huge stones of warehouses and the palaces of the merchant-princes, and scraped the very rock. Tyre is dead; whatever inhabited ruins or temporary revivals may survive – and such are assumed by the predicted "spreading of nets" – the proud, imperial mistress of the seas had, like Capernaum, gone down to the pit (Ezek. 26:20), the dark underworld of the dead.'

After the subjugation of Syria and Phoenicia, Alexander turned to Philistia, precisely as foretold by Zechariah. Four of the principal cities of Philistia were mentioned (Ashkelon, Gaza, Ekron and Ashdod – see also Zeph. 2:4). Gath was not mentioned and may have been destroyed already. The fact that the mighty city of Tyre had fallen struck fear into them. It has been said that 'Philistine arrogance in their independence, their nationality and their prowess was proverbial,' but the cities of Philistia were now to be humbled and brought low. Their rulers were slain since Alexander's policy was to destroy tributary monarchies and to maintain a consolidated empire: fallen kings were, therefore, replaced by his own appointed governors. Ashkelon was to be left without inhabitant, Gaza was to lose its ruler, Ekron was to experience grief and the dashing of her hopes, and Ashdod was to be occupied by a mongrel race. The predictions were completely fulfilled. Ashkelon was depopulated, Gaza was destroyed after five months' siege and its ruler was killed by being dragged through the streets, Ekron certainly had her hopes dashed to the ground: Tyre was not, as she had hoped, an obstacle to the imperial forces, yet the prophet foretold that one day Ekron would be like a Jebusite. Amos had also declared, 'I will send a fire on the wall of Gaza, which shall devour its palaces: and I will cut off the inhabitant from Ashdod, and him that holds the sceptre from Ashkelon, and I will turn my hand against Ekron: and the remnant of the Philistines shall perish, says the Lord God' (Amos 1:8; see Zeph. 2:4). Ashdod was to be occupied by aliens and the whole region fell a prey to the Macedonians.

The pride and arrogance of Philistia was brought down to the dust but, at the same time, God indicated that He had purposes of blessing for the Philistines. He declared that He would remove the blood out of his mouth and his abominations from between his teeth. 'The Philistines were considered by the Jews as an unclean people,' writes Barnes (op. cit., p. 73), 'partly because they were uncircumcized (Jud. 14:3), partly because they ate food forbidden by the law, particularly the blood of sacrificial victims (cf. Ps. 16:4; Ezek. 33:25). Here the promise is that some of the Philistines (the inhabitants of Ekron) shall be purified and united as proselytes to Israel.' Calvin takes the view that verse 6 visualizes Philistia as a wild beast from whose jaws the prey which he is devouring is torn, but this is not really tenable. The word 'abominations' is consistently used as a symbol of idols or idolatry, and this seems to be the significance here. Jehovah intended to cleanse the Philistines of their idolatry and to fit them for incorporation into Israel. A remnant would be saved and would become part of Judah. Because of its geographical situation, close to the borders of Israel, Ekron was chosen as an illustration: she would be like the Jebusites whom David incorporated when he captured their stronghold of Zion (2 Sam. 5:6). Philistia, in general, would become a chieftain (or chiliarch, the head of a thousand) in Judah. This prediction has not, of course, yet been fulfilled and it presumably awaits the coming of Messiah.

Judah might well have been fearful at the approach of the great conqueror, but Jehovah declared that He would protect His temple (and inferentially the city) against any attack by the Macedonian army. He would encamp around them to be their shield from the armies passing to and fro and to ensure that no oppressor passed through the land any more. It is remarkable that, although the Macedonian armies passed and repassed the city of Jerusalem, they left the temple and God's people unharmed. According to Josephus (*Antiquities* XI, 8:3), after taking Gaza and razing it to the ground, Alexander advanced quickly towards Jerusalem. He demanded the payment of tribute which the Jews had customarily paid to the Persians. Jaddua, the high priest, refused to break his agreement of loyalty to Darius. In a dream given to the high priest, God encouraged him to faith and confidence, and instructed him to fling open the gates and to go forth, clad in his priestly robes, with all the priests in his train, and all the people clad in white garments. Jaddua obeyed and the gates were opened, and the Macedonians gazed upon the remarkable spectacle. When Alexander saw the procession and the high priest in his gold-embroidered robes and his mitre with its golden plate of holiness, he fell upon his face and worshipped. Parmenio asked him the reason for his obeisance. The youthful ruler replied that he had seen the high priest in a dream at Dios, clad in purple and scarlet, and attended by priests in white. Alexander entered the city with Jaddua, and the latter acquainted him with the prophecies of Daniel which appeared to be relevant to himself and his empire. The Macedonian was so impressed that he accepted the message as Divinely given and spared the Jews. There is an implication in verse 8, of course, of a Divine protection extending beyond the period of the Macedonian invasion and realized more fully in a day still to come. God will yet protect His own land from all who threaten to invade and overrun it.

'Now have I seen with My eyes', said God. Not only did He observe every act, but He could read the motives and could, in addition, peer into the future. The most pertinent significance is perhaps that He took notice in order to intervene if He considered it necessary.

CHAPTER 14

The Coming of the King

At the close of the preceding sub-section, Jehovah had declared that He had seen with His eyes, tacitly implying that He was aware of the afflictions and trials of His people and that He would interpose on their behalf when the time came, as He did when Israel suffered at the hands of their taskmasters in Egypt (Exod. 3:7). He provided protection for them in the days of Alexander the Great, but will yet prove Himself to be their deliverer in the fullest possible sense. The next sub-section accordingly announced the event through which complete deliverance might have come (and was only delayed because of the Jews' rejection of the Deliverer). 'Sion is called upon,' says Perowne (op. cit., p. 113), 'to welcome with exultation her just and lowly King, who comes to her in humble state (v. 9), whose kingdom of peace shall cover all the land and embrace all nations (v. 10), and who, mindful of His covenant with her, shall give deliverance to the captives of Israel (vv. 11, 12). Using them, now once more an united nation, as the instruments of His warfare (v. 13), Himself fighting for them and manifesting Himself as their Protector (v. 14), He will make them victorious over all their enemies (v. 15), and will promote them to safety and honour (v. 16), magnifying His "goodness" and his "beauty" in the prosperity with which He crowns them (v. 17).' We have quoted *in extenso* because Perowne's summary is so concise and yet complete.

There can be no dubiety about the identity of the One described in verses 9 to 11. Even Rashi, the well-known Jewish commentator, said, 'It is impossible to interpret it of any other than King Messiah', and the Christian, with the pages of the New Testament open to him, unhesitatingly identifies the 'king' with the Lord Jesus Christ.

'Rejoice greatly, O daughter of Zion. Shout, O daughter of Jerusalem. Behold, your king comes to you. He is just and showing himself a Saviour, lowly and riding on an ass and on a colt, the foal of an ass. And I will cut off the chariot from Ephraim and the horse from Jerusalem, and the battle bow shall be cut off. And he shall speak peace to the nations. And his dominion shall be from sea to sea, and from the river to the ends of the earth. As for you also, because of the blood of your covenant, I have sent forth your prisoners out of the pit wherein is no water. Turn you to the stronghold, you prisoners of the hope. Even today do I declare that I will render double to you; when I have bent Judah for me, filled the bow with Ephraim, and raised up your sons, O Zion, against your sons, O Greece, and made you as the sword of a mighty man. And Jehovah shall be seen over them. And his arrow shall go forth as the lightning: and the Lord Jehovah shall blow the trumpet, and shall go with the whirlwinds of the south. Jehovah of hosts shall defend them. And they shall devour, and subdue with sling-stones. And they shall drink, and make a noise as from wine; and they shall be filled like bowls, as the corners of the altar. And Jehovah their God shall save them in that day as the flock of his people: for they shall be as the stones of a crown, lifted on high over his land. For how great is his goodness and how great is his beauty: Corn shall make the young men thrive, and new wine the maids. Ask of Jehovah rain in the time of the latter rain; so Jehovah shall make lightnings, and give them showers of rain, to every one grass in the field' (9:9–10:1).

Having implied that He would constantly watch over His people, God now called upon Zion and Jerusalem to exult and shout for joy. Their King was coming to Jerusalem. But the Jews had no king at that time and were subject to a Gentile power; no Jew had borne the title of king after the exile. Here was One who had been designated God's King centuries earlier (Ps. 2:6), the One of whom the earlier prophets had spoken (Isa. 9:6, 7), and for whom the nation waited in anticipation. This King was just or righteous, completely unlike the capricious and unjust rulers of history, and He was the dispenser of salvation. If deliverance had virtually been assured in the earlier half of the chapter, here was the One by whom it would come.

It might have been anticipated that the King would come in glory and splendour, with regal pomp and dignity, but He was described as lowly or humble, in complete contrast with the proud and arrogant rulers of this world (cf. Phil. 2:5–7). Illustrative of His character was the beast that carried him. From the days of Solomon onwards, the poor might ride upon an ass, but kings and nobles were always borne by a horse. Yet this King was to come, riding on an ass and on a foal of she-asses. This was precisely how He came, for the prophecy was literally fulfilled at the first advent of our Lord (Matt. 21:1–9; Mark 11:1–10; Luke 19:28–38; John 12:12–15). His entry into Jerusalem on that first Palm Sunday was on a beast of burden – not even a full-grown animal, but an untrained and unbroken colt – to be hailed with Hosannas by the crowds which, the same week, were to yell for His blood. Lange says that the prophecy 'presents a person in whom the greatest grandeur, magnificence, power and influence are associated, without confusion or contradiction, with the greatest humility, gentleness, poverty, suffering and weakness. No judge, king, or ruler of any sort in all Jewish history ever united in his character or experience these two extremes. None was so lowly, none so exalted. None without arms spoke peace even to his own people, much less to the heathen, and least of all to the entire known world. It is true of only one being in all human history that he had not where to lay his head and rode upon an ass, and yet acquired a limitless dominion over land and sea.' The Deliverer came, but His own people were so blind that they rejected Him.

Chambers (op. cit., p. 71) says that the Jews had a 'fable that the ass created at the end of the six days of creation was the same which Abraham saddled when he went off to offer Isaac, and which Moses set his wife and sons upon when he came out of Egypt; and that this distinguished animal was to bear the Messiah. . . . It is supposed that the prophecy in some way gave rise to the foolish statement of Tacitus, that the Jews consecrated the image of an ass in the inmost shrine of their temple, and hence probably arose the calumny upon the early Christians, who were often confounded with the Jews, that they worshipped an ass's head – a fable which Tertullian takes the trouble to repeat.'

As happened so often in the prophetic Scriptures, Zechariah apparently ignored the whole of the period between the two advents of our Lord and turned immediately to what would occur at and immediately prior to the second advent. Since the king was also the generalissimo of the forces, the announcement of the coming of the King would at once have conjured up, in the minds of those who heard (or subsequently read) the prophecy, the picture of war and the advent of a captain to lead his people into battle and victory. They were disabused of this potential misunderstanding, however, for Jehovah declared that He would cut off the chariot from Ephraim (i.e. Israel) and the horse from Jerusalem (metonymically Judah), the battle bow would be cut off and the King would speak peace to the nations. Israel and Judah had been separate kingdoms from the rebellion of Jeroboam in the tenth century B.C. (1 Kings 12:16, 17). Often at war with one another, horse, chariot and battle bow were the apt symbols of their means of offence and defence. But these were to be cut off and, by inference, the two kingdoms to be reunited (cf. Ezek. 37:16–22). Messiah would bring salvation, but not by military weapons. His victory would be won by the word of His mouth, and He would proclaim peace, not only to Israel, but to the Gentiles as well. Patently this has not yet been fulfilled and the prophecy obviously anticipated the Second Advent.

Moreover, the dominion of God's King, the Messiah, was not to be restricted to Israel and Judah. He would reign in peace over the whole world. In the picturesque language of the prophecy, his dominion would be from sea to sea (an idiom for the whole earth) and from the river (i.e. the Euphrates, the future boundary of the promised land – see Gen. 15:18) to the ends of the earth (Ps. 72:8). Jerusalem would be the focal point of His rule, but all nations would be subject to Him and own His sovereignty. This is the day for which creation had waited. This is the day so long foretold by prophet and seer, when the unhewn stone will pulverize the Gentile colossus and then expand to fill the whole earth (Dan. 2:34, 35).

Still addressing Zion and Jerusalem, Jehovah promised the return of the exiles to their own country. His covenant with His people had been ratified by blood. It is not clear whether the reference was to the Sinaitic covenant (Exod. 24:8), the Palestinian covenant (Deut. 30:1–10), or the Davidic covenant (2 Sam. 7:14–17), or even possibly to the Abrahamic covenant (Gen. 15:1–21) which preceded the nation as such. Ratification by blood was essential if any covenant was to be binding upon the parties to it. Because of the blood of the covenant God promised to deliver Zion's prisoners from the waterless pit. It was often the custom to confine prisoners or criminals in a cistern or dry well (Gen. 37:24; Jer. 38:6), and the prophecy visualized the exiles as symbolically imprisoned in similar fashion. Some commentators see an allusion to the Maccabean period in the description, while others claim that it is a reference to the great tribulation of a future day. Like many other Biblical prophecies, it is probably susceptible to more than one fulfilment, but its final fruition doubtless still lies in the future.

The sufferers were exhorted to turn to the stronghold, or, as Barnes renders it, 'Return to Him who is a stronghold', i.e. to God himself (Joel 3:16). These exiles hoped for early release and were, therefore, appropriately described as 'prisoners of the hope' (i.e. the hope of freedom or the Messiah Himself as the hope of the ages). David Baron (op. cit., p. 323) points out that 'Zech. 9:12 is the only place in the Hebrew Bible where the word for hope has the article. It is, therefore . . . not any hope, or general hope, that the prophet speaks about, but the special hope of Israel, the hope which sustained him through all the years of patient expectation. The centre and essence of it is the Messiah, and the great promised material and spiritual redemption which He was to accomplish.'

That very day, Jehovah declared, He would recompense to them double. The law stipulated that the firstborn son should receive a double portion of his father's property, but the term is also sometimes employed of the punishment meted out (Exod. 4:22; Deut. 21:15–17; Isa. 40:2; Jer. 16:18). In the context the implication is that double blessing would be the lot of God's people.

The concluding verses of the chapter are usually interpreted as a description of the struggle for independence in the times of the Maccabees (175 to 43 B.C.), which commenced in a determined resistance to the attempts of Antiochus Epiphanes to impose the idolatrous Greek worship upon the Jews. The verses may also be regarded, however, as anticipative of the coming of Messiah in glory and power to deliver His people. Certainly God portrayed Himself as a mighty warrior directing His power against Javan. He took Judah as His bow, treading upon it as He bent it, and He used Ephraim as the arrow to fill the bow. He raised up Zion's sons like a spear to attack the sons of Javan (or Greece), and wielded Zion as the sword of a mighty man. 'The mighty man,' as another remarks, 'did not use His sword until the enemy had been put to flight by the bow; the sword was used in the pursuit; it was, therefore a symbol of victory.' The figurative language, therefore, portrayed various stages in the conflict, but throughout it was clear that God was fighting on behalf of His people, albeit using them as His weapons.

In a number of Assyrian and Persian pictures of reliefs of a battle, the patron god or goddess is shown in the air above the human combatants, affording them supernatural help and protection in the fray. Jehovah declared that He similarly would be seen above His people and that His arrow would go forth as lightnings. The picture was that of a storm, the thunder-blasts serving as the sound of His trumpet, and the lightning as the swift flight of the arrow. God would sweep on with His people and with the whirlwind of the south: the Negev and Teman were regarded as the home of the whirlwind (Isa. 21:1; Hab. 3:3); it was from that direction that the fearful storms came and they were frequently pictured as the instrument of the Divine wrath (Ps. 83:15; Jer. 23:19). His fury would be irresistible in that day: nothing could withstand the vehemence of His anger.

The prophecy declared that Jehovah would protect His people as with a shield. They would be completely enveloped by His guard, and the enemy's attacks would consequently be ineffective and unavailing. Like a wild beast Judah would devour or consume their assailants and would tread them down like sling-stones. Sir George Adam Smith suggests that they will subdue the foe with sling-stones, and Barnes argues that the reference is to hailstones by which God crushes the attackers, but the purport seems rather that they will trample their foes under foot as fallen sling-stones are trampled in the mud and mire. They would treat the enemy as mere pebbles from the brook.

The victors (although Barnes suggests that it is the Lord's arrows) would metaphorically drink the blood of the defeated as a wild beast does the blood of its victim as it devours its flesh.

Victory would be complete and in their exuberance they would hilariously celebrate their triumph with boisterous shouting, like those who were intoxicated with wine. In the temple service, the blood of the sacrifices was caught in the sacrificial bowls and then sprinkled upon the corners of the brazen altar (Lev. 4:7, 18, 30). The prophet pictured the victors in the guise of the sacrificial bowls, filled with the blood of the slain: bespattered with the blood of the gory battle, they were like bowls filled with the blood of the sacrifice. Most commentators treat the imagery as pertinent to the Maccabean victories, but the experiences of that period can scarcely exhaust the significance completely, and there is a great deal to be said for the view that the complete fulfilment of the passage will not occur until the coming of Messiah as the great warrior to deliver His chosen people.

This is possibly confirmed by the statement that God would save His people 'in that day' (a phrase with an eschatological significance). This implied more than deliverance from their foes, for the promise was that He would save them as 'the flock of His people'. Isaiah declares that in a coming day, 'He shall feed his flock like a shepherd: he shall gather the lambs with his arm, and carry them in his bosom, and shall gently lead those that give suck' (Isa. 40:11). The implication of both prophets is that regeneration must have been effected and that there had been a restoration of communion with God. They could hardly otherwise be referred to as His flock. Like the sparkling jewels of a crown, honoured and glorified, would they be lifted up as an ensign over the land (cf. Mal. 3:17). Barnes argues that Zion is the crown and its inhabitants the glittering jewels. An 'ensign' was the indication of the presence of the king. The victorious Jews were to shine as precious gems and themselves to serve as Messiah's ensign as evidence of His return. Clearly, therefore, the prophecy looked beyond the times of the Maccabees to the Second Advent of our Lord.

Contemplating the wonder of the Divine purpose and the extent of His interest in His people, the prophet burst out with an expression of praise of God. (The words obviously cannot apply to Israel, as is sometimes suggested.) 'How great is His goodness! How great is His beauty!' Pusey quotes Osirius as commenting, 'The prophet, borne out of himself by the consideration of the Divine goodness, stands amazed while he contemplates the beauty and Deity of Christ: he burst out with unwonted admiration! How great is His goodness, who to guard His flock shall come down on earth to lay down His life for the salvation of His sheep! How great His beauty, who is the brightness of the glory and the image of the Father, and comprises in His Godhead the measure of all order and beauty.' Goodness is repeatedly ascribed to God (e.g. Ps. 31:19; 145:7) and beauty is ascribed to the Messiah (Isa. 33:17; Ps. 45:2, 3).

Corn would make the young men flourish, and wine would have a similar effect upon the young women. The prophecy was patently anticipating the material prosperity of the millennium and not merely that which ensued after the Maccabean victories. The blessings of the golden age would cause youth to flourish spiritually and materially. Barnes (op. cit., p. 78) says, 'Resolving the poetic parallelism we may paraphrase as follows, "corn and new wine shall bring forth fruit, even young men and maidens". Renewed fertility of the soil will result in a growth of the population, both of young men and of maidens.' Corn was necessary to provide the staff of life, and wine symbolized the joy and happiness of the people. All needs would be met and happiness would be Judah's portion.

One of the greatest needs in the Middle East is of water, and rain is regarded as a tremendous blessing. The early rain falls in the autumn and is 'essential for the sprouting of the newly-sown grain'. 'The latter rain falls in March and serves to swell the grain then coming to maturity' (Perowne). God promised Israel that the result of obedience to His commands would be the bestowal of the first rain and the latter rain (Deut. 11:14; see also Joel 2:23). One of the punishments inflicted upon Israel and Judah for their sinfulness was the withholding of rain (e.g. 1 Kings 17:1): when they repented the rain was restored (1 Kings 18:45). Now He bid them to seek the gift of rain, the latter rain. If they did, He would cause lightning to induce the clouds to yield up their moisture and the abundant rains to fall. He would give them showers of rain to produce 'grass in the field' (Gen. 1:29). The copious downpour would supply their need in full. All they had to do was to ask. The same circumstances apply today and if the blessing of the outpouring of the Divine Spirit is to be experienced, we must ask. The outpouring of the rain was, of course, typical of the outpouring of the Spirit which is yet to be experienced by Israel (Joel 2:28), and the same blessing is the need of the believer today. But the infilling of the Spirit is available to the one who desires it and will yield to God for it.

CHAPTER 15

The Only Answer

Zech. 10 is closely connected with the previous chapter and it is impossible to detach verse 1 from chapter 9. The prophet had clearly indicated that all blessings and temporal benefits were derived from God and that His people's hearts should, therefore, be turned to Him. But they had sought help from other sources and it was with this that the prophecy went on to deal.

'For the idols have spoken vanity, and the diviners have seen a lie and have told false dreams. They comfort in vain. Therefore they went their way as a flock; they were troubled because there was no shepherd. My anger is kindled against the shepherds and I will punish the goats; for Jehovah of hosts has visited his flock the house of Judah, and will make them as his goodly house in the battle. From him shall come forth the corner, from him the nail, from him the battle bow, from him every oppressor together. And they shall be as mighty men, who tread down their enemies in the mire of the streets in the battle. And they shall fight, because Jehovah is with them, and the riders on horses shall be confounded' (10:2–5).

Judah had resorted to the idols or *teraphim*, i.e. the household gods (Ezek. 21:21; Jud. 17:5; Hos. 3:4). The *teraphim* were actually small images of the divinities of the home, and were apparently consulted for guidance regarding proposed actions (Ezek. 21:21). They figured largely in the idolatry of the northern kingdom of Israel, but were also found in Judah, although their use was Divinely condemned (1 Sam. 15:23; 2 Kings 23:24). But they were in use in Babylonia at quite an early date, and Rachel stole those of her father Laban (Gen. 31:34), since possession of them was linked with leadership of the family and they also ensured her husband's ultimate entitlement to her father's property. When Jacob reached Shechem, he commanded that all *teraphim* and other idols held by the members of his company should be surrendered (Gen. 35:2–4). If Judah had consulted the *teraphim*, it was to no purpose, for they only uttered falsehoods (or wickedness). Their guidance was worthless.

The people had, therefore, consulted soothsayers or diviners, but this was equally ineffective. Their divination, to quote J. D. Davis, was an 'attempt to read the future and utter soothsaying either by a kind of inspiration or afflatus (Acts. 16:16), or else by means of signs. In the latter sense, it includes augury or foretelling the future by means of natural signs, such as the flight of birds, the disposition of the liver (Ezek. 21:21); hydromancy or foretelling from the appearance of water poured into a vessel or of objects dropped into the water (Gen. 44:5); foretelling by casting lots (Ezek. 21:21); and astrology or the determination of the supposed influence of the stars or the destiny of a person or a nation (cf. Isa. 17:13). The Hebrews also included in divination necromancy or foretelling the future by calling up the spirits of the dead and conversing with them (1 Sam. 28:8). The Babylonians were famous for their liver divination (hepatoscopy).' A scrutiny of an animal's liver was supposed to reveal the god's will through the manner in which that organ was fashioned. But Zechariah declared that what the diviners had seen was untrue. They had simply uttered vain or empty dreams and their comfort was as empty as the air (or, to use a modern idiom, only 'hot air').

In consequence, the people went their way like sheep. Because the grass was quickly consumed by the sheep or burnt up by the sun, it was necessary for sheep to be continually led to fresh pastures by the shepherd. Judah resembled the sheep in their wandering but, unlike the usual flock, they were without a shepherd and, therefore, strayed to their own hurt. Chambers (op. cit., p. 78) remarks, 'Israel having lost its native rulers, fell under the power of the heathen governors, here styled shepherds and he-goats.' Jehovah declared that His anger was burning against these brutal and self-appointed shepherds – the nations which had oppressed His people – and He would punish the he-goats, i.e. the rulers of the heathen nations (Isa. 14:9). Those who afflicted His people would eventually suffer at His hand. The complete fulfilment of the prophecy must, of course, await our Lord's return in judgement, although a partial fulfilment may have been seen in the past. It was appropriate, therefore that the prophecy should announce that Jehovah of hosts had visited His flock, the house of Judah. The great Shepherd would come to His shepherdless people. And, in that day, He would make them 'as his goodly horse in the battle'. As Moore puts it (op. cit., p. 160), 'God will visit His flock in mercy and make each one, instead of a timid sheep, to be a war-horse, decked for battle.' The final conflict was coming and the oppressors would be routed by the mighty warrior, but He would employ Judah as the strong and powerful steed to carry Him to victory.

If the clash of arms seemed already to be sounding, the prophet now painted the most reassuring picture of the sufficiency of the Messiah for all Judah's needs and in all her circumstances. Zech. 10:4 is perhaps one of the most remarkable portrayals of the Messiah. The fourfold picture of corner-stone, tent peg, battle bow and exactor was graphic and its significance far-reaching. That One was to come 'from him', i.e. out of the people of Judah as, in fact, actually occurred.

Out of Judah, Messiah came forth as the corner, or corner-stone. The corner-stone was the principal stone of the foundation, and the security of the whole superstructure virtually depended upon the stability and sureness of the foundation-stone. It was laid at the corner of the building, at the point at which two walls would be constructed. If it was unstable or badly laid, the whole of the building was jeopardized. Its stability was of fundamental importance. An earlier prophet said, 'Behold I lay in Zion for a foundation a stone, a tried stone, a precious corner-stone, a sure foundation' (Isa. 28:16). The apostle Paul declared that the Church as a whole and the believer personally were 'built upon the foundation of the apostles and prophets, Jesus Christ himself being the chief corner-stone' (Eph. 2:20). With that One as the foundation, none need fear or be in doubt. There was absolute security. Messiah was the corner-stone.

The corner-stone, however, was not only the foundation-stone, but also the headstone. As already mentioned in chapter 7, that headstone had been literally rejected by the builders of the temple of Zerubbabel's day and it had become a stumbling stone or 'rock of offence'. But when the builders sought a stone to fill the vacant place at the top of the corner, the only one that would exactly fit the gap was the stone which they had rejected and over which they had stumbled, and with songs of triumph they brought out the rejected stone and placed it in its appointed place as head of the corner. There is no dubiety about the interpretation, for our Lord specifically applied the type to Himself (Matt. 21: 42), as did also the apostle Paul (Rom. 9:32, 33; 1 Cor. 1:23). He is both foundation-stone and top-stone. The whole building is held together by and in Him. This is just as much the case today as for Judah centuries ago.

Out of Judah also was to come the nail or tent peg. The reference was not to the stake driven into the ground, to which the ropes were fastened, but to the large wooden peg inside the tent or, in later days, fastened to the wall of the house. Upon that 'nail' would be hung all the domestic utensils of the tent. It bore the load. In Oriental houses subsequently, the nail became a number of ornamental pegs around the walls, the treasures of gold and silver and objects of beauty being suspended therefrom. The nail not only carried the burdens of the household, but also its beauties and glories. The Messiah was to become the great burden-bearer for His people, but additionally, all the glory should hang upon Him. When Hezekiah's steward, Shebna was deposed from his position, Eliakim, the son of Hilkiah, succeeded him, and God declared that He would 'fasten him as a nail in a sure place' and that they would 'hang upon him all the glory of his father's house, the offspring and the issue, every small vessel, from the cups to all the flagons'. The prophet saw figuratively every tent door flung open and from the surface of every burnished vessel, hanging from the nail, the reflection of the morning sun. All the glory of the tent was hung from the nail (Isa. 22:20–25). Messiah was to be not only the bearer of all the burden of life, but the One on whom the glory hung. As a result of the practical significance attached to the nail, it became used metaphorically of the head of the household, because all other members of the family were dependent upon him.

Thirdly One was to come forth as the battle bow. A strip of elastic wood or metal with a cord stretched between its two ends, the bow was used for both hunting and war (Gen. 27:3; 48:22). It was in general use among the nations at an earlier date, but was still regarded as the symbol of armed might. The little country of Judah had no military strength and would be quite unable to face the attack of a hostile power. So Messiah was presented as the Divine archer, who would uncover His bow (Hab. 3:9) and direct His arrows into the hearts of His enemies (Ps. 45:4). Zechariah evidently anticipated the moment of Divine interposition in the affairs of men of which the Apocalypse later gave so much more detail (Rev. 19:11). Judah was incapable of confronting the foe, but she was not called upon to fight the battle. Another would stand beween her and the forces of the enemy, and the battle would be fought and the victory won by a Captain from above. How true for the Christian also that he fights not his own battles: the mighty Warrior stands beween him and the foe and the victory is won, not by the arm of flesh but by the power of God.

From Judah also was to issue forth 'every oppressor (R.S.V. "ruler") together'. The oppressor was the exactor of tribute and Unger argues that *noges* invariably has an evil connotation and the reference must, therefore, be to oppressive rulers and tyrants. Feinburg also, in *God Remembers*, p. 188, maintains that 'the reference cannot possibly be to the Messiah because *yahdaw* ("together") proves definitely that more than one oppressor will go forth'. On this basis, the implication would be that, through the presence and power of Messiah, all oppressors would unitedly depart from Israel. Barnes (op. cit., p. 80) puts a different complexion on it in his comment, 'The *noges* is one who exacts from the people (1) taxes (cf. 2 Kings 23:35); (2) forced labour (cf. Exod. 3:7); (3) military service, as in the present passage. Here the "exactors" correspond to the "scribes" of 1 Macc. 5:42, who had to see that none of the army of Judas Maccabaeus shirked the fighting. The prophet says that all the army of Judah, commander, subordinate officers, rank and file, and provost marshal, come from Jehovah. All authority is from Him.' The text is certainly as susceptible to this interpretation as to that of Unger and Feinberg.

David Baron, who frankly admits that the constructon of the sentence in the original is unusual and peculiar, gives the following possible renderings of the verse, 'Out of him (Judah) shall come (or go) forth every exactor (in the sense of absolute ruler) together,' while he quotes Prof. Aaron Pick as rendering the text in his *Literal Translation of the Twelve Minor Prophets* as, 'From him the corner, from him the nail, from him the battle bow, yea, from him shall come forth He that conquereth all together.' But then Baron says (op. cit., pp. 355, 356), 'In rendering the words *khol noges yachdaw* "every ruler together" or "he that will exercise all rule", I am guided more by the context and obvious sense than by strict principles of Hebrew grammar. It seems to me that, as the first terms in this verse undoubtedly refer to the Messiah in allusion to utterances about His person and mission by the former prophets, so must this last clause also. Certain it is that the Messiah at His Second Coming shall gather up in Himself all authority and rule.' This seems the most logical interpretation. The One to whom all tribute is due (and who should receive it from willing hearts and not by compelled exaction) shall come forth from Judah. In that day, the rejected Christ will be acknowledged as the supreme ruler in every sphere – celestial, terrestrial and infernal – and every knee shall bow to Him and every tongue acknowledge His lordship (Phil. 2:10, 11; Eph. 1:10, 20–23).

Judah was totally unprepared for the military conflict which faced her. But Jehovah was to raise up a leader in the person of the Messiah, who would be all-sufficient for the nation's need. With the realization of His presence and the inspiration of His leadership, the weakling became strong, and the army of Judah became valiant heroes, trampling underfoot their enemies in the mire of the streets. The description given can scarcely be restricted to the period of the Maccabees, although it was presumably partially fulfilled then, but essentially it seems to relate to the end time when God's people are confronted with the greatest opposition and danger of their history. But in that day, they will fight in confidence because Jehovah is with them. No doubt as to the ultimate result enters their mind. Victory is assured. The cavalry of the mighty Gentile forces are overthrown. The proud cavalry of Antiochus was, in fact, trampled down by the irresistible force of the Maccabean army. 'As soldiers trample through mud and mire,' writes Smith, 'as their bespattered uniforms, as well as their bloodstained clothes, proclaim their valiant bravery, so the soldiers of the Lord go on. They fight, not in their own strength, but in the power of the Lord who is with them, so that even the riders on horses, the most feared and most powerful of their foes, shall be confounded and put to shame.'

The prophetic Word indicates that, at the end time, the land of Israel will suffer invasion from the south and from the north and possibly also from the east, and that an attempt to deliver may well come from the west. The picture painted, even in Zechariah's last chapter, is of a nation in her extremity and only delivered by the Second Advent of Christ. It is difficult to pinpoint precisely when this particular prophecy may be fulfilled, but one fact that emerges is that God has not utterly forsaken His people and that one day He will once more intervene on their behalf.

CHAPTER 16

The Nation's Restoration

If the interpretation of the earlier verses of Zech. 10 is restricted to the period of the Maccabees, there is obviously a considerable gap between them and the fulfilment of the verses that follow. If, however, the first five verses are regarded as applicable to the period of the Second Advent, the remainder of the chapter follows logically, since it clearly describes the repatriation of the whole nation at the coming of Christ.

'And I will strengthen the house of Judah, and I will save the house of Joseph. And I will bring them back to place them, for I have mercy on them, and they shall be as though I had not cast them off: for I am Jehovah their God and I will hear them. And they of Ephraim shall be like a mighty man, and their heart shall rejoice as with wine. Yea, their children shall see and be glad; their heart shall rejoice in Jehovah. I will hiss for them and gather them; for I have redeemed them: and they shall increase as they have increased. And I will sow them among the peoples: and they shall remember me in far countries. And they shall live with their children and shall return. I will bring them again also out of the land of Egypt, and gather them out of Assyria; and I will bring them into the land of Gilead and Lebanon, and place shall not be found for them. And he will pass through the sea of affliction and will smite the waves in the sea. And all the depths of the Nile shall dry up: and the pride of Assyria shall be brought down, and the sceptre of Egypt shall depart. And I will strengthen them in Jehovah; and they shall walk up and down in his name, says Jehovah' (10:6–12).

Visualizing the possibility of the whole of the nation as being once more reunited, God announced that He would make the house of Judah strong and would save the house of Joseph, i.e. Ephraim or Israel. Nearly three centuries earlier, Israel had been deported by the Assyrians (2 Kings 17:6) and just over a century later, Judah had been deported by the Babylonians (2 Kings 24:14–16; 25:11). God had given Israel a bill of divorce (Isa. 50:1): He treated her as no longer His. But now His mercy reached out once more to His people and He purposed to treat them as though He had never rejected them. He would not only save Israel, but repatriate them. He would bring them back to cause them to dwell (inferentially in their own land). It is usually argued that, since the partial restoration from Babylon, Israel and Judah have been regarded as one nation with one hope and destiny. Chambers (op. cit., p. 80), for example, says, 'The prediction of the return of Ephraim in this chapter has been sometimes cited as evidence that the ten tribes are still somewhere existing as a separate community, and as such are yet to be restored to their own land. But this is an error. The words of the prophet were fulfilled in the period to which he refers. Many of the transplanted Ephraimites fell away from the faith and became absorbed in the heathen by whom they were surrounded, but many who remained true to Jehovah, joined their fortunes with those of their brethren of Judah. Their common calamities softened and, at last, obliterated the old feelings of enmity towards each other. Jerusalem became again the central point of the whole nation, and while not a few actually shared in the restoration, others who remained in exile, yet adhered to the second temple, aided it by their gifts, and often attended the yearly festivals. Hence all the latter were comprehended under the term, the *Diaspora* (Jas. 1:1). In the New Testament there are repeated allusions to the twelve tribes, conveying the distinct impression that the inhabitants of Palestine in our Lord's day represented both parts of the nation.'

Certainly it seems probable that some members of the northern kingdom of Israel returned to the land with the exiles of Judah. It is also clear that the ten tribes of Israel do not exist as a distinct and recognizable community today, although again, members of the ten tribes may well be among those who are commonly described as Jews. Many theories have been propounded regarding the 'lost ten tribes' and they have been identified with the Nestorians, Afghans, Red Indians, etc. and British-Israelism claims to have found links with Britain and the U.S.A., but a positive identification of Israel as a separate body, distinct from Judah, has not proved possible. Yet there are not lacking Scriptures which clearly indicate that Israel is to be restored to her own land and reunited with Judah (e.g. Isa.

27:12; 43:5–7; Ezek. 28:25, 26; 37:16–23; Amos 9:14, 15). Zechariah plainly envisions the repatriation of the whole of the twelve tribes, reunited as one rejoicing people. Jehovah's compassion will reach out to His own and He will hear their cries. He is 'Jehovah their God and will hear them'.

Lest there should be any doubt, the prophecy stated plainly that Ephraim or Israel, although still in dispersion, would be like a mighty man and would exult in jubilant joy. Judah's future might seem assured, but Ephraim's was equally definite. Exhilarated as though by wine, they will then rejoice in Jehovah. The apparently impossible will have become an achieved fact – and solely through the hand of God. No evanescent joy is theirs, for another generation, their own children, will see the wonder-working of Jehovah and will be so stirred by the amazing happenings that they will share in the general rejoicing.

It is usually maintained that Zech. 10:8–12 forms an explanation of the manner in which the ten tribes will be restored to the land, but this is open to question and it seems probable that the verses relate to the whole of the twelve tribes, or 'the house of Judah' and 'the house of Joseph', visualized now as one company. Obviously there are many of Judah to be regathered as well as those of Israel. Jehovah announced that He would personally summon His people from their world-wide dispersion. In Matt. 24:31, however, our Lord disclosed that, at His coming, His angels would be sent to 'gather together His elect from the four winds, from one end of heaven to the other'. The regathering, therefore, will not take place until the return of Christ to earth.

The summons, described by our Lord as with a trumpet, is described by Zechariah as the shrill whistle or the piping used by the apiarist to summon his bees and unite his swarm. Previously God had gathered hostile nations against His people by 'hissing' or whistling for them, and like the countless numbers of the insect world the messengers of His vengeance had assembled (Isa. 7:18, 19; 5:26, 27). Then the shrill call was one denoting impending judgement. Now he would summon His people in similar fashion, but for their blessing. Since the same word was used in both cases, there may be a tacit implication that the first call having achieved its purpose, the second call would be equally unfailing. Indeed, God explicitly stated that He would gather them for He had redeemed them. They were to be ransomed, not only from banishment and exile, but from their sins and iniquities. They were His. Moreover, despite all their experiences, they would increase phenomenally, just as they did in Egypt before the exodus.

The people had been scattered, but their disciplinary dispersion had not been for the ultimate loss. Seed was sown by scattering it over the land, not that it might be lost but, on the contrary, that it might produce a far more abundant harvest. Similarly, God's people had been sown among the nations in order that they too might prosper and multiply (see also Hos. 2:23). The time would come when, in their dispersion in far countries, their minds would return to former things and they would remember Jehovah. Their revival and turning to God at His call would be permanent and complete, for their children would be associated with them. The spiritual regeneration barely hinted at in Zechariah is, of course, plainly described in Ezek. 37:14.

Isa. 11:11 declared that Jehovah would recover the remnant of His people a second time from Assyria, Egypt, etc. Zechariah made the same statement – that He would bring them again out of Egypt and gather them out of Assyria (see also Hos. 11:11). Gesenius opines that 'Egypt and Assyria are mentioned here in place of the different countries into which the Jews were scattered.' Moore (op. cit., p. 166) also considers that 'Egypt and Assyria are taken as types of all the lands of their dispersion, the one being the first great oppressor of the chosen people and the other among the last, and the one lying on the north whilst the other lay on the south. Hence they are here taken merely as types of the universal dispersion.' Although, in the past, captives have been carried to both the south and to the lands in the north, they have since been scattered to almost every part of the world, and Moore's suggestion is possibly the only satisfactory explanation. The typical use of the names of Egypt and Assyria would, as Chambers remarks (op. cit., p. 79), be 'neither unnatural nor unusual. Egypt was the first oppressor of the convenant people, and Assyria was the final instrument of overthrowing the ten tribes, and the two terms might well be combined as a general statement of the lands of the dispersion' (cf. Isa. 27:13; 10:24; 11:11, 16; 19:23; 52:4; Hos. 11:11).

On their return to the land, however, they would be allotted

Gilead and Lebanon, i.e. the northern part of Palestine on both sides of the Jordan, previously occupied by the ten tribes. Gilead on the west of the Jordan, was originally occupied by Reuben, Gad and Manasseh: the area from Gilead to the Lebanon range in the north is not very extensive, but was the extent of the territory promised under the various covenants with Israel (Gen. 15:18; Deut. 30:3–5; etc.). But so numerous will the people be that the space will be inadequate to accommodate them (cf. Isa. 49:20, 21).

When Israel made their exodus from Egypt, they were faced with the obstacle of the sea, but the Almighty made a passage for them through the sea (Exod. 14:27–31). Nothing was to prevent their future restoration to the land. God declared that He would pass through the sea of affliction and smite the waves in the sea. The reference is not, of course, to a literal sea; the term is used metaphorically of any obstacle which might confront them. Just as God had opened a passage through the waters in the earlier history of His people, so He would now quash all opposition and remove all obstacles. In their journey into the promised land, Israel passed over the river Jordan dryshod (Josh. 3:14–17). Similarly (but again only in a metaphorical sense presumably) the river Nile would dry up so that nothing might hinder the course of God's people. The overweening pride of the northern oppressor would be brought down, and the sceptre (or rod) of Egypt, the symbol of Egyptian authority and restraint, would no longer be able to oppress (cf. Isa. 9:4) or to obstruct the people of Israel. Everything would be swept away in that day to give them a clear passage on their return home.

Nor was this the end. As Unger (op. cit., p. 186) pertinently remarks, 'the phenomenal regathering of His people out of their world-wide dispersion and settling them in their own land, at the same time removing every obstacle in the way of their return, is only part of the Divine undertaking for them. In their own land they shall experience a copious outpouring of the Spirit that will enable them to do marvels in God's name.' God declared that He would strengthen them and that they should walk up and down in His name. Barnes sees this as signifying that their whole life and conduct will be in accord with the name of their God, but Baron undoubtedly is more to the point in his assumption that the allusion is rather to their acting as the messengers and representatives of Jehovah dispensing the blessings of Messiah's gospel among the nations. This was God's original purpose for His people, but in a future day, it will be fully realized and Israel will be a missionary nation among the peoples of the earth.

It is patently possible to allegorize the specific promises made to Israel and Judah. The attempt to evacuate these predictions of their literal meaning and to apply them spiritually to the church is poor exegesis and poorer interpretation. Indeed, the concluding words of the chapter, 'says Jehovah', seem to set the Divine seal upon the explicit statements made and to assure their fulfilment.

CHAPTER 17

The Northern Scourge

In view of the spiritual insight he shows and the structural comparisons he makes, David Baron's introductory remarks to Zech. 11 are well worth quoting *in extenso*. He says (op. cit., pp. 375, 376), 'The 11th chapter stands in the same relation to the verbal prophecies which make up the second part of Zechariah, as the 5th does in relation to the first part of the visions. . . . In the first part we have first a series of five visions which in various symbols set forth "the good and comfortable words" of promise concerning restoration, enlargement, and temporal and spiritual blessing which God has yet in store for the land and the people of Israel. But to complete the prophetic forecast of the future, . . . the obverse side of the picture, which sets forth a yet future apostasy and judgement, had to be presented. This is done in the visions of the flying roll and the ephah, in the first of which we hear God's great curse pronounced against sin; and in the second we see its banishment from His own land and presence "to the land of Shinar" – the original place of rebellion and apostasy against God – where it shall meet with its final doom. In the 6th chapter, however, we emerge again from the dark valley of sin and apostasy, and we are shown in the symbolical transaction there set forth how, in spite of it all, Israel's Messiah will yet be crowned, and sit and rule upon His throne, and be a priest upon His throne; and how, not only Israel, but "they that are far off", shall find a place in the glorious temple which He shall build.

'And thus it is also with the second part. First, we have a series of verbal prophecies, which are full of promise of future restoration and blessedness; and then, in order to prevent a carnal misuse of the promises of salvation on the part of the godless majority in the nation, and also as a hint that the full realization of the promises was, from the prophet's point of view, in the yet distant future, we are suddenly in the 10th chapter brought to the precipice of a tremendous gulf of national apostasy and consequent judgement. But even from this deep abyss we shall emerge again in the last three chapters, where Israel's national repentance and mourning over Him whom they have sold for thirty pieces of silver, and "pierced", are depicted for us in inspired language, which reads almost like history instead of prophecy. And the end and blessed issue of Israel's national conversion and reunion with their Messiah will be that "Jehovah will be King over all the earth".'

The comparison is significant. At the same time, it seems almost incredible that apostasy should take place when the promises of God shine so brightly before the gaze of His people.

Zech. 11 is the second section of the first 'burden of the word of Jehovah', and it is concerned primarily with the rejection of the Shepherd, whose coming had been foretold in Zech. 9. The first sub-section of three verses, painting the impending devastation of the land in the imagery of a tremendous storm, form a prelude to what follows. The verses portray in symbolic language the story of the invasion of the land from the north – in the view of some by the Chaldeans, when they captured Jerusalem, destroyed the people and carried away captives to Babylon. But it is more probable that the prophecy looked on to the future rather than back to the past. The Assyrian and Babylonian invasions of an earlier day were past history. It is more likely that what is pictured is the ruthless savagery of Antiochus Epiphanes and the Syrian forces in a later day – and possibly even an invasion which still lies in the future.

'Open your doors, O Lebanon, that the fire may devour your cedars. Wail, fir tree; for the cedar is fallen; because the mighty goodly ones are spoiled. Wail, O you oaks of Bashan; for the impenetrable forest is come down. There is a voice of the wailing of the shepherds; for their glory is spoiled: a voice of the roaring of young lions; for the pride of Jordan is spoiled' (11:1–3).

The 100 miles long Lebanon range of mountains runs parallel to the coast and its western flanks sweep down to the sea, leaving a narrow coastal plain for the cities of Tyre, Sidon, Beirut, etc. The height of its peaks varies from 6,000 to 10,000 feet. Its white limestone and the snow that caps its peaks for much of the year have given it its name (white). Its slopes were covered with forests of gigantic cedars and lower down with an abundance of fir or cypress trees, the lowest being covered with vines. Lions, leopards and other wild beasts found a shelter in its woods. An invasion from the north might well come along the Phoenician littoral on its west.

Apostrophizing the mountain range as though it was a mighty fortress, the prophet called upon Lebanon to throw open its doors to admit the devastation that was threatened. Resistance was pointless, because the doom was inevitable. Then, in startling imagery, he presented the picture of a tempest of unprecedented fury. It tore down the steep mountain paths of Lebanon – open to its tornado-like force – setting the massive cedars on fire with its lightnings and utterly consuming the proud monarchs of the forest. As the conflagration rapidly spread, the prophet dramatically declared that the cypresses wailed as they saw the fate of the cedars and realized what would be their own. If the impenetrable forest of Lebanon had been consumed, the oaks of Bashan howled in fear and despair at their own impending doom.

The Chaldean forces had swept down in such a fashion (Isa. 14:8), Sennacherib of Assyria had threatened to do the same (Isa. 37:24). The enemy had literally felled the cedars of Lebanon in earlier days and his reckless torch had set fire to the forests of fir and cypress. The picture painted may not relate only to the past: there may be an allusion also to the horrors of a future invasion – evidently far more destructive and far-reaching than any which has preceded it – when the hordes of the northern confederation of powers sweep down through Palestine to plunder and destroy (Dan. 11:40–45). History has a habit of repeating itself and Biblical prophecies often have more than one fulfilment.

Bashan was located on the east of the river Jordan and ran to the border of the Arabian desert. Davis says, 'It is a broad fertile plateau, of volcanic formation, and well adapted for pasture. It was celebrated for its cattle (Ps. 22:12; Ezek. 39:18; Amos 4:1), and for its breed of sheep (Deut. 32:14). It was known also for its oak trees (Isa. 2:13; Ezek. 27:6; Zech. 11:2). Forests of evergreen oak still survive.' Bashan's forests had been deemed strong and inaccessible, but the fire swept over the oaks of Bashan and consumed them.

The desolating tempest which had wrought such havoc on the highlands now travelled down to the lowlands and from the plateau to the plain. Here there was fresh tragedy and as the fire reached the rich pasture lands, the shepherds were called upon to wail for the loss of their very livelihood. The fields in which they had their sheep and cattle were now scorched and useless. They howled lugubriously as they saw the spoiling of their 'glory' (the pasture lands).

Another howling came from the Jordan valley, for 'the pride of Jordan' (Jer. 12:5; 49:19; 50:44) was also desolated. The banks of the river were fringed with close thickets, a luxuriant jungle of willows, tamarisks, and cane, in which lions made their covert. As the fire swept over the banks of the river and devoured the thick growth, the roaring of fierce young lions was heard, furious at the destruction of both their lairs and their food. The whole of the country was in flames: everything had been destroyed. History apparently records no literal fire or storm so completely devastating as having occurred in the part.

It would be difficult to find a more terrible picture of utter desolation. Whether it is intended to be taken literally or figuratively, the description is of an appalling devastation. Many expositors have attempted to see typology in the mountains and plains, the various trees and the animals but, as Leupold (*Exposition of Zechariah*, p. 206) pertinently remarks, 'A literal interpretation . . . carries us far enough. For surely, if the land is so completely devastated as is here described, all greatness and great men will also have been involved in the universal ruin.' Smith, on the other hand, sees no doubt regarding the interpretation. He says, 'A ruthless army, who knows no pity, who delights in destruction, murder and oppression, is advancing against Judah and Jerusalem. As the vultures gather from afar around the carcass, so the enemy forces are seen gathering about Jerusalem. Since the context refers to the days of Messiah (v. 12), the reference is to the siege and destruction of Jerusalem and the devastation of the entire land by the armies of Rome, A.D. 70 and 71. The Jewish nation will be rejected by the Lord because of its rejection of Him and His Shepherd.'

That no mere natural happening is portrayed is evident from the opening words, 'Open your doors, O Lebanon'. They constitute a command by God to prepare no resistance, but to make way for the destruction that is impending. Plainly what is envisaged is a judgement directed by the Almighty Himself. Human or natural instruments may be employed but the ultimate cause is the will of God – patently in judgement upon a guilty and rebellious people. 'Our God is a consuming fire.' Another writer aptly remarks, 'The agency of God is still exerted as really in the continued existence of the universe, as in its original creation.' He has not abdicated His sovereignty of the universe and none sins against Him with impunity.

Moore is convinced that the reference is to the judgement which fell after the rejection of the Lord Jesus Christ, and consequently applies the scene to the Roman invasion of the first century. He writes (op. cit., p. 171), 'The metaphor describes the storm of invasion, bloodshed and oppression that should roll over Palestine after the glorious Maccabean era, and before the coming of the Messiah. The designation of Lebanon and Bashan belong to the metaphor, and not to the fulfilment, being designed to set forth by the usual course of such storms the track of this tempest, and hence it is not necessary for us to show that any invasions actually came by the way of the Lebanon. The reference is to that desolating storm of civil war that caused the calling in of the Romans, whose legions swept like a whirlwind of steel over the land, and finally prostrated every vestige of independent authority, from the cedar of Lebanon to the lowliest cypress, from the peaceful shepherd to the lionlike spirit that refused to be subdued, and humbled the whole land beneath the mighty power of Rome. It was this state of deep prostration that constituted the dark hour before the dawn, the fulness of time on the arrival of which the great shepherd was to come.'

If this interpretation is accepted, the next section of Zech. 11 furnishes an explanation of the cause of the fearful judgement described in this first section. The crime committed by the people was so heinous and of such a character that the judgement had to fit the crime. Even if the primary fulfilment occurred nineteen centuries ago, however, the description given seems extremely appropriate to the dark period of trouble for the land which still lies ahead. The significance is not entirely exhausted by what has already occurred in the past.

CHAPTER 18

Rejection of the Shepherd

The remainder of Zech. 11 is devoted to the rejection of the Good Shepherd but, for convenience, may perhaps be divided into three sub-sections: (1) the flock of slaughter (vv. 4–7a); (2) the two staves (vv. 7b–14) and (3) the foolish shepherd (vv. 15–17).

'Thus says Jehovah my God, Feed the flock of slaughter; whose buyers slay them and hold themselves not guilty: and they that sell them say, Blessed be Jehovah, for I am rich: and their own shepherds pity them not. For I will no more pity the inhabitants of the land, says Jehovah: but, lo, I will deliver each man into the hand of his neighbour, and into the hand of his king. And they shall smite the land, and out of their hand I will not deliver them. So I fed the flock of slaughter, verily the poor of the flock' (11:4–7a).

As happened not infrequently in the ministry of the prophets (e.g. Ezek. 4:1–17; 5:1–4), Zechariah was called upon by Jehovah to enact a parable in order that the Divine message might be conveyed to the people. He was directed to act in the capacity of the shepherd of a flock. Dressed in the appropriate garb and carrying the two staves which a shepherd would normally carry, he assumed the charge of the flock. In his capacity of a shepherd, he was, of course, representing the line of true shepherds which culminated in the Good Shepherd our Lord Jesus Chtist. It is occasionally suggested that the parable was merely an inward vision and not an actual occurrence, but there is no sound reason for treating it as anything else than a genuine commission intended to be acted out before his contemporaries.

He was to 'feed' or 'shepherd' the flock. The word used implies far more than mere feeding and it includes the concept of the full range of the shepherd's duties – feeding, leading, guiding, nursing, protecting, healing (cf. Ps. 23:1–6). The sheep he was to care for were termed 'the flock of slaughter' (cf. Ps. 44:22; Jer. 50:6, 7, 17), i.e. those destined to be butchered. The reference was, of course, to the prophet's own people, and it is usually suggested that the description appropriately delineated, by inference, the conditions at the time of the Roman siege and capture of Jerusalem. It seemed then as if nothing could save the Jews from their fate and, in fact, over 1,100,000 Jews perished at the fall of Jerusalem and another half a million during the war and the siege. They certainly seemed to be a flock for slaughter. It is questionable, however, whether the Romans alone can be regarded as the slaughterers in view of the following verse, since it was the buyers or possessors who slew the sheep.

The flock had been treated as mere chattels, to be bought or sold without compunction and without any consideration for the animals themselves. Those who bought or possessed them slew the sheep without any sense of wrongdoing, or guilt. Barnes (op. cit., p. 85) considers that 'the allusion is to abuse of justice; the "buyers" are the oppressors who give bribes; "they that sell them" are the judges who accept the bribes'. Moore (op. cit., p. 173) maintains that 'by the buyers and sellers are meant the Romans, who used the Jews, as they did all their conquests, as mere merchandise, making from them the greatest possible gain for themselves'. As already suggested, this does not seem completely tenable, however, in view of the words attributed to the sellers in the same verse. E. Henderson (*The Book of the Minor Prophets*, p. 420) suggests more consistently that 'by the buyers and sellers of the Jewish people, we are not to understand the Romans, but their own unprincipled teachers and rulers'.

Those who sold the sheep turned complacently to Jehovah and blessed Him for the profit made on the sale and for the fact that they were becoming rich. They had the barefaced hypocrisy to thank God for the ill-gotten wealth derived from unmercifully fleecing the sheep and then selling it. The fact that they attributed their wealth to Jehovah appears a clear indication that those alluded to were themselves Jews rather that Romans, since the latter would never have given even a nominal recognition to Jehovah.

Pathetically the prophecy stated that 'their own shepherds pity them not'. The shepherds are deemed by most expositors to be 'the civil and ecclesiastical rulers of the Jews', and it is claimed that what is depicted is the 'extortion and treachery in which the Pharisee and Sadducee wrung from the unhappy people what the Roman had failed to extort, and both combined thus in spite of their mutual hate in this work of shameless robbery'. If the period referred to prophetically was the first century A.D., the avaricious exploitation of Jew by fellow-Jew implied in Zechariah was demonstrated to the full. The tragedy was that this ruthless exploitation was Divinely permitted as a means of punishment. As Moore remarks (op. cit., p. 173), 'although once they who oppressed the covenant people would be guilty and so treated by God, now the sins of the people were such that these oppressions were righteous punishments, and their agents, therefore, not guilty for the execution itself, however they might be for the mode and motives with which they performed it'.

Even more tragic was that God Himself had no more pity for the inhabitants of the land. Their experiences were no more than they deserved. When they rejected the Messiah and cast Him out, they exposed themselves to the pitiless wrath of the God against whom they had sinned (cf. Ezek. 8:18). Their wickedness was of such a character as to be completely intolerable to Him, and their misery was the direct result of their conduct. They were delivered, every man into the hand of his neighbour and into the hand of his king. They chose a thief and a murderer in preference to Christ, and God surrendered them to their fate. Civil war and internal discord raised the hand of Jew against Jew. Factions bitterly opposed one another in bloody strife. In their rejection of Christ, they had cried, 'We have no king but Caesar' (John 19:15). God delivered them into the hand of the one whom they acknowledged, and the Romans destroyed their city and temple. As the prophecy foretold, the land itself suffered. In the words of Zechariah it was to be beaten to pieces: in fact, it was laid completely waste. There was no help and no hope, for the God of Israel had declared that He would not deliver His people. Accordingly, they paid the price of their crimes in bloodshed and death. Their protection had been withdrawn and they were exposed to the merciless assaults of the heathen.

Nevertheless, even in that dark hour of Israel's extremity, there were still some who retained their loyalty to Jehovah. They had been left untended and uncared for by the shepherds who should have cared for them, and had been cruelly treated and oppressed by those who had assumed authority. God aptly termed them the poor of the flock, although one translator renders the phrase, 'the most miserable of sheep'. But that faithful remnant were not lost to the eyes of the Great Shepherd, and on His behalf, Zechariah declares that he shepherded the poor of the flock, who also seemed destined for slaughter. He deemed it his duty to fulfil the terms of his appointment and to afford them his special care.

A shepherd normally carried a strong stick or club, with which to beat off any wild beasts who sought to attack the flock, and also a crooked staff to facilitate the retrieving of sheep which had fallen into difficult places and could not recover themselves. The psalmist referred to these as the Lord's rod and staff (Ps. 23:4). It is with these and with the rejection of the shepherd that the next sub-section is primarily occupied.

'And I took unto me two staves; the one I called Beauty, and the other I called Bands. And I fed the flock. Three shepherds also I cut off in one month, for my soul was weary of them, and their soul also loathed me. Then said I, I will not feed you: that that is dying, let it die; and that which is being cut off, let it be cut off; and let the rest eat every one the flesh of his fellow. And I took my staff, Beauty, and cut it asunder, that I might break my covenant which I had made with all the peoples. And it was broken in that day. And so the poor of the flock that gave heed to me certainly knew that it was the word of Jehovah. And I said to them, If it be good in your eyes, give me my wages; and if not, forbear. So they weighed for my wages thirty pieces of silver. And Jehovah said to me, Throw it to the potter: the goodly price at which I was valued by them. And I took the thirty pieces of silver and threw them into the house of Jehovah to the potter. Then I cut asunder my other staff, Bands, that I might break the brotherhood between Judah and Israel' (11:7b–14).

Zechariah took the usual two staves of the shepherd and named one Beauty (or grace) and the other Bands (or union). They were indicative of the Divine purposes for Israel and Judah in the Good Shepherd. He came to establish peace and to display grace and to reunite completely the peoples of the twelve tribes. So equipped the prophet cared for the flock.

Then Jehovah suddenly announced that He would cut off three shepherds in one month. He had become impatient with them and a mutual antipathy had developed, for they, on their part, loathed or abhorred Him. There has been a great variety of interpretations of the three shepherds. Ewald suggested that the reference was to the last three kings of Israel, viz. Zechariah, Shallum and Menahem (2 Kings 15:8–17). Marti and others saw in them the high priests, Lysimachus, Jason and Menelaus; Sellin substituted for these the names of Simon, Menelaus and Lysimachus. Perowne put the alternative of Antiochus Epiphanes, Antiochus Eupator, and Demetrius I, in the times of the Maccabees. The consensus of opinion, however, is that it was none of the many persons whose names have been suggested, but the three offices of king, priest and prophet. As one writer points out, 'These three classes are mentioned together in Jer. 2:8, 18 as perverters of the nation and causers of its destruction.' These consequently were to suffer.

They were to be cut off (i.e. disavowed rather than destroyed) 'in one month'. It is not possible to identify a literal period of thirty days in which what was prophesied occurred, and the import seems rather to be a short period than a specific time. Unger considers that it was 'the period of culminating unbelief just before the national leaders crucified our Lord and thus sealed the fate of the Jewish state'.

The prediction of Zechariah that the leaders would be disavowed by God because He had lost patience with them is extremely pertinent to the events subsequent to the crucifixion of Christ. He had grown weary of their perverse impenitence which culminated in their rejection of His Son, but it was equally true that they had no real desire for Him. As Smith says, 'Their soul abhorred Him. They thought Christ their political liberator. When He taught them the true nature of His kingdom, they abhorred Him and turned away in disgust and hate. . . . They rejected Christ as Messiah. Finally they were rejected as a nation by God and never again as a nation had their own divinely appointed kings, priests and prophets.'

In the light of what had happened, the shepherd declared that he would no longer feed the flock. His care of them would be withdrawn and he would abandon them to their fate. He would not intervene to save them. Those who were dying would be left to die without help or sympathy. The scattered or straying would be left to follow their wayward desires and, in all probability fall into pits or crevices or be lost on the hillside: no one would seek them. The rest would be left to devour one another. The three forms of calamity mentioned, as Chambers points out, are death by natural causes, plague or famine; violence at the hand of foreign foe; and intestine discord. The words were evidently applicable particularly to the remnant who escaped from the destruction of Jerusalem (cf. Jer. 44:27). Many would be destroyed by the Romans, but the country would be torn by dissension and domestic strife, various opposing factions bitterly quarrelling and attacking one another and thereby weakening the strength of their own country. Instead of pacifying his sheep and healing their wounds and supplying their needs, the shepherd surrendered them to the cruelty and oppression of their foes. This was certainly evidenced after the fall of the city and the temple.

Then the shepherd took his staff, Beauty, and deliberately broke it in pieces before the eyes of the people and declared that God had broken the covenant which He had made with the nations (cf. Hos. 2:18). The latter possibly referred to the restraint laid upon the nations that Israel might be safeguarded. Now, that restraint was to be removed and the grace shown to God's people was to be ended. 'This staff,' says Barnes (op. cit., p. 86), 'stands for all the institutions which Jehovah gave to Judah for advantage – the kingdom, the priesthood, the temple with its services, etc. All were broken.' The covenant with the peoples is sometimes said to relate to the twelve tribes and not to other nations. (The word used is *ammim*, peoples, and not *goyim*, nations or Gentiles. The word *ammim* is used for the tribes of Israel in Deut. 33:3; Hos. 10:14, etc.) Whatever interpretation is placed upon the details, the broad significance is clear. For their rejection of His Son, God will give up His people to a righteous retribution and will no longer be known as their defender and protector. When the staff was broken, the 'poor of the flock', who had retained their trust in God through difficult circumstances would acknowledge that all these events were the fulfilment of God's word.

Completely abandoning his office of shepherd, Zechariah (clearly under Divine direction) asked for the wages due to him but, at the same time, indicated his indifference to the reaction of the owners of the flock. 'If it be good . . . and if not forbear.' Chambers (op. cit., p. 85) saw in the words an implied final appeal to all of the people, 'the form of the inquiry, which arises simply to ascertain whether they are willing to acknowledge and appreciate his pastoral care, shows that it must be addressed to the whole flock'. On the other hand, the words emphasize the mutual aversion which now existed between the shepherd and the flock.

In reply to the shepherd's request, the people meticulously weighed out thirty pieces of silver as a suitable measure of reward. Their action could scarcely have been more insulting. Thirty pieces of silver was the amount stipulated by the law as the payment to be made in respect of a slave gored by an ox (Exod. 21:32). Such was their estimation of the value of the faithful service of the shepherd. In the New Testament counterpart of Zechariah's prophetic allegory, the people paid the same amount of thirty pieces of silver to the traitor Judas for his betrayal of his Master. So contemptuous were they in their evaluation of His worth.

Jehovah viewed the insult paid to His servant as an insult paid to Him personally. Thirty shekels was the wage of one of the lower grades of workers and, in Eccles. 38:29 ff. potters were included in manual workers who were not 'sought for in the council of the people'. A magnificent price, God ironically termed it, and directed the prophet to throw it to the potter. 'Throw it to the potter' was a proverbial phrase, contemptuous of the worth of the article concerned, and comparable with our own phrase, 'Throw it to the dogs.' Zechariah obeyed the Divine instruction and threw the silver to the potter in Jehovah's house. Köhler says, 'The sum is just large enough to pay a potter for the pitchers and pots which he furnishes, and which are thought of so little value that men are easily comforted for the breaking of any by the thought that others can be readily obtained in their stead.' This does not explain, however, the contemptuous spurning of the sum expressed in the command to cast or throw it to the potter.

Hengstenberg argues from Jer. 18:2; 19:2 that a potter was employed in the temple, whose workshop was in the valley of Hinnom, because the most suitable clay was found there. The valley was deemed an unclean place because of the idolatrous worship of Moloch formerly carried out there, and because of the defilement of it by Josiah with carrion, bones, etc. (2 Kings 23:10). He claims that the throwing of the thirty pieces of silver to the potter (whose workshop and himself were unclean because of their location) was simply a renewal of the symbol of the smashing of the potter's vessel in Jer. 19:10, 11 and a fresh pledge of God's purpose to punish. Ingenious although his theory is, there is no evidence of a special potter associated with the temple nor of a potter's workshop in Hinnom.

When Judas Iscariot repented of his treachery, he flung down in the temple the thirty pieces of silver which he had received as the blood money. Since dishonourable money could not remain in the temple (Deut. 23:18, 19), and could not be put into the treasury, the priests used it to purchase 'the potter's field, to bury strangers in' (Matt. 27:3–7). Commenting on the events, the Evangelist added, 'Then was fulfilled that which was spoken by Jeremiah the prophet, saying, And they took the thirty pieces of silver, the price of him that was valued, whom they of the children of Israel did value, and gave them for the potter's field, as the Lord appointed me' (Matt. 27:9, 10). There is no Biblical record of Jeremiah having said this and the story seems to find its closest parallel in Zech. 11:12, 13. In a note in *The Harvester*, Prof. F. F. Bruce suggests, as a possible explanation 'that in the source from which the Evangelist drew the quotation, Zech. 11:13 was combined with a quotation or quotations from Jeremiah (whether Jer. 18:2, 3 along with 32:6–15, or Jer. 19:1–13, or some other passage), and that the earlier of the two prophets alone was mentioned by name. You have something similar in Mark 1:2, 3 (R.V., etc.), where the words "As it is written in Isaiah the prophet", introduce two quotations, the former of which is from Malachi and only the latter from Isaiah. Some have emphasized that the prophecy quoted in Matt. 27:9 is there said to have been *spoken*, not *written*, by Jeremiah; but "that which was spoken" is Matthew's regular wording in introducing his "formula-quotations", without any distinction between speaking and writing (see e.g. Matt. 2:17; 4:14; 8:17; 12:17).'

Zechariah says nothing about the purchase of a field, but Jeremiah, who says nothing about the betrayal, states that

Jehovah appointed him to buy a field (Jer. 32:6–8) as a solemn guarantee by God that fields and vineyards would again be bought and sold in the land. Jeremiah had regarded that as impossible, but God assured him that nothing was too hard for Him. The potter's field would not have been purchased by the priests if the threefold divine assurance had not been fulfilled (Jer. 32:15, 43 f.). This potter's field was one of the fields God had in mind when He spoke to Jeremiah. On the other hand, Jeremiah says nothing of another circumstance closely connected with the purchase of the potter's field, viz. that it was to be bought for the thirty pieces of silver, the price of Him that was valued, nor that this money would be cast into the temple. These details were added by Zechariah. Matthew combines both prophecies and names Jeremiah because he was the major prophet and had foretold what Matthew particularly intended to stress, the purchase of the field (see also A. Edersheim's *Life and Times of Jesus the Messiah*, pp. 573–6).

Then Zechariah broke in pieces his other staff, Bands, to signify the breaking of the brotherhood between Judah and Israel. The rupture between the shepherd and the flock inevitably involved the end of fraternal unity as well. Unger (op. cit., pp. 201, 202) writes, 'The prediction made here involves the utter breaking up of those social and religious ties that had always united the people of Israel into a solidly knit-together people. This fearful dissolution of their own national solidarity was occasioned largely by the internal dissensions brought about by the conflicting parties which prevailed among them, which at the last pitilessly pitted brother against brother, and was more cruel and destructive than the suffering occasioned by the besieging Romans. . . . God would no longer interpose to check disunifying factors.'

The good shepherd having been rejected, the worthless shepherd was now presented in his place.

'And Jehovah said to me, Take to you yet the equipment of a foolish shepherd. For, lo, I will raise up a shepherd in the land, who will not visit those that are cut off, neither will seek the scattered, nor heal that which is wounded, nor feed that which stands firm. But he will eat the flesh of the fat sheep, and tear their hoofs in pieces. Woe to the worthless shepherd who forsakes the flock! The sword shall be upon his arm, and upon his right eye: his arm shall be utterly withered and his right eye shall be utterly blinded' (11:15–17).

Zechariah was called upon to enact another parable before the people. Once again he took the shepherd's equipment – presumably rod, crook, bag, pipe and knife – and now acted the part of an unfaithful shepherd. As such, he was typical of another shepherd who was to be raised up in the land, who would callously ignore the needs of the flock and his responsibilities to them, and would instead show an insatiate rapacity and gluttonous desire for gain. Commentators have seen in this foolish shepherd a picture of Pekah, Hosea, Menahem, Zedekiah, Herod, the Romans, etc., but Chambers is possibly more to the point when he interprets him as 'the ruling power in whomsoever vested'. It was the duty of the ruler to care for his subjects; he was their shepherd. A good ruler was concerned about the welfare of his people. A bad ruler offered no care or protection and was absorbed only by his own interests. The foolish shepherd, of whom Zechariah was symbolical, would not visit or search for the wandering sheep who had strayed from the flock and who might well be in danger. He would not solicitously seek the young who might need special care. He would be indifferent to the needs of the wounded and enfeebled. He would not provide food for the robust, who stood firmly when the weakling fell (cf. Ezek. 34:4–6). In blatant unconcern, he would pay no regard for their need, but instead would display insensate and diabolical greed and aggressive gluttony. Like a voracious beast, he would feast upon the plump animals instead of nourishing and feeding them, and would even tear their hoofs to pieces to extract any goodness for himself.

Chambers sees in the imagery a representation of the suffering of Judea at the hands of the Roman Empire at and after the siege of Jerusalem. He writes (op. cit., p. 88), 'The ruin of the place and the people was overwhelming. Scarce any siege in the history of the world was attended with such cruelties and horrors as preceded and followed the fall of Jerusalem. There was a deliberate and energetic effort to exterminate the race. The whole power of the Roman Empire was brought to bear upon this one province. . . . And the subsequent history of the Jews for many centuries illustrated in the same manner the symbol of Zechariah. Their rulers were evil shepherds, mock shepherds. Giving nothing, they exacted everything. They taxed, they pillaged, they oppressed, they insulted, habitually and on principle. The Jew was an outcast without any right, and when tolerated it was only as a sponge to be squeezed when it was full.' Our Lord declared that He was the good shepherd, but that the hireling would flee from danger and leave the sheep to their fate (John 10:11–14). The good shepherd was rejected, but 'another shall come in his own name', He said, 'him you will receive' (John 5:43). When His people yielded Him up, they cried, 'His blood be on us and on our children' (Matt. 27:25). They suffered for their self-appointed malediction four decades later but they have continued to suffer through the centuries. Although there have been many precursors, the false shepherd, who will come in his own name, has not yet appeared, but when this Antichrist appears, the Jews will receive him to their suffering and loss.

'Woe to the worthless shepherd,' said Jehovah. It is said that the words were a proverbial taunt by shepherds against an incompetent or unworthy fellow-shepherd, but in this case it was the pronouncement of judgement too. The one who had so shamefully neglected his charge and abused the flock was to be punished. The sword would smite his arm and his right eye: his arm would wither and his eye would be blinded. His eye should have watched over the sheep, and his arm should have protected them. His fate was, therefore, a fitting one. Chambers comments (op. cit., p. 88), 'The worthless shepherds, who battened like vultures on the wretched flock of Judea, the haughty Romans who inflicted the divine judgements upon the apostate and incorrigible nation, were themselves in turn exposed to a righteous retribution.' The threatened judgement did, of course, actually occur in history. 'Rome,' says Moore (op. cit., p. 185), 'like some old lion who had ravaged for many years, when his eye grew dim and his arm grew weak, lay down to die. And it was precisely then that, in addition to the internal feebleness, there came upon them, from the forests of the north, the sword, and thus were literally fulfilled the terms of this passage.' Rev. 19:20 reveals that another, the worthless shepherd, of whom the others were all typical, will one day also meet with his fate at the hand of Christ. Zech. 11:17 is to have more than one fulfilment.

CHAPTER 19

Deliverance and Repentance

The first 'burden of the word of Jehovah' (chapters 9 to 11) is concerned primarily with the first advent of the Messiah, culminating in His rejection as the good shepherd and the nation's acceptance of Antichrist, the worthless shepherd. The long parenthesis between these two events, during which God has been calling out the church, is not indicated in Zechariah. A hint that a hiatus would take place was given in Dan. 9:26, but again no clear statement was given respecting it (see *The Climax of the Ages*, by F. A. Tatford).

The second 'burden of the word of Jehovah' (chapters 12 to 14) is concerned principally with the second advent of the Messiah and the effect of His return upon the people and the land. Like the first burden, it is divided into two parts, chapters 12 and 13, dealing with the deliverance and conversion of Israel, and the second part, chapter 14, dealing with Messiah's advent in glory and power. Sixteen times in the three chapters the phrase 'in that day' occurs (12:3, 4, 6, 8, 9, 11; 13:1, 2, 4; 14:4, 6, 8, 9, 13, 20, 21). It seems clear that the reference is to 'the day of Jehovah', in which the judgements of God will be poured out and the unparalleled troubles of the great tribulation will be experienced until the climax is reached in the return of the Lord Jesus Christ to earth. A comparison of the occurrences of the phrase show that it has an eschatological significance.

The first sub-section (12:1–9) describes the future siege of Jerusalem in the most graphic manner.

'The burden of the word of Jehovah concerning Israel. Says Jehovah, who stretches forth the heavens, and lays the foundation of the earth, and forms the spirit of man within him, I will make Jerusalem a bowl of reeling to all the peoples round about. And upon Judah also shall there be affliction in the siege against Jerusalem. And in that day will I make Jerusalem a burdensome stone for all the peoples: all that burden themselves with it shall tear themselves to pieces, though all the nations of the earth be gathered together against it. In that day, says Jehovah, I will smite every horse with terror, and his rider with madness. And I will open my eyes upon the house of Judah, and will smite every horse of the peoples with blindness. And the chieftains of Judah shall say in their breast, The inhabitants of Jerusalem are my strength in Jehovah of hosts their God. In that day will I make the chieftains of Judah like a pot of fire among the wood, and like a torch of fire among sheaves; and they shall devour all the peoples round about, on the right hand and on the left. And Jerusalem shall be inhabited again in her own place, even in Jerusalem. Jehovah shall also save the tents of Judah first, that the glory of the house of David and the glory of the inhabitants of Jerusalem might not be magnified above Judah. In that day shall Jehovah defend the inhabitants of Jerusalem. And he that is feeble among them at that day shall be as David; and the house of David shall be as God, as the angel of Jehovah before them. And it shall come to pass in that day, that I will seek to destroy all the nations that come against Jerusalem' (12:1–9).

The second burden is stated to be concerning Israel, although the details which follow relate to Judah, Jersusalem and the royal house. The view is usually taken that the name is used here in a religious, and not in a political, sense and that it relates to Judah, Jerusalem and such members of the northern kingdom as had associated themselves with Judah.

God declared that He who spoke stretches forth the heavens, lays the foundation of the earth, and forms the spirit of man within him. The heavens are sometimes described in the Old Testament as though they were a curtain (Ps. 104:2) and at other times as though they were a metal plate or firmament (Gen. 1:6). In this case, the analogy of the curtain was employed. It is significant that the verbs used imply a continued action and not a completed event. As Moore (op. cit., p. 189) says, 'The Bible is ignorant of that philosophy which teaches that God has created the universe and wound up its machinery like a clock and then left it to run on by its own inherent energies. From moment to moment He is exerting His power in maintaining the movements of visible things.' 'Every day,' says Hengstenberg, 'He spreads out the heavens, every day He lays the foundation of the earth, which, if it were not upheld by His power, would wander from its orbit and fall into ruin.' Again, the reference to the forming or fashioning of man's spirit does not as Keil remarks, refer merely 'to the creation of the spirits or souls of men once for all, but denotes the continuous creative formation and guidance of the human spirit by the Spirit of God'. It is the mighty omnipotent and omniscient God who utters the burden.

Immediately prior to Christ's return to earth, it is evident that there will be an invasion of the land of Israel, and Zech. 12 pictures all nations gathering against Jerusalem. The prophet gives no clue to the identity of the nations concerned, but Dan. 11 indicates that attacks upon the land will come from both the south and the north. The treaty mentioned in Dan. 9:27 will presumably cause an intervention from the west. In addition, Rev. 16 implies that there will also be an invasion from the east. The circumstances and period seem to be identical with those in chapter 14:2, except that in the latter case, God states that He has gathered the nations against Jerusalem, whereas the earlier reference implies that they will gather of their own volition.

The gathered nations will reach out to seize the city and to take possession of all its treasures. Zechariah portrays the city as a bowl of wine which they eagerly quaff. But Jehovah has converted the contents into an intoxicating draught, which causes them to reel and stagger like a drunken man, confused and discomfited (cf. Isa. 51:22, 23; Ps. 75:8). The word cup or bowl, which is used, was also employed of the bowl in which the blood of the paschal lamb was caught (Exod. 12:22), but it has been argued that the word *saph* means 'threshold' and not 'cup' and that what was envisaged was the quaking threshold of the city, its tremors being due to an earthquake which disturbed the whole area. This, of course, would be in agreement with Zech. 14:4.

The grammatical construction of the latter part of verse 2 is difficult and it has been deduced from the literal rendering, 'and also upon Judah shall be in the siege against Jerusalem', that Judah will ally herself with the hostile forces attacking the metropolis. But, as Keil observes, 'There is no indication whatever of Judah's having made common cause with the enemy against Jerusalem; on the contrary, Judah and Jerusalem stand together in opposition to the nations, and the princes of Judah have strength in the inhabitants of Jerusalem (v. 5), and destroy the enemy to save Jerusalem (v. 6).' The rendering we have given, 'and upon Judah also shall there be affliction in the siege against Jerusalem', seems more appropriate than the A.V. and others.

It was the custom for athletes to develop their strength by lifting and throwing heavy stones. God declared that He would make Jerusalem a burdensome stone, which the nations would essay to lift, only to find it too heavy to handle. In consequence, the stone would slip and grievously injure those who thought it was an easy burden to hold. They would be badly wounded. Some expositors have seen in the illustration a reference to the heavy mortality of labourers engaged in the transport of huge stones for the building or embellishing of cities, and the implication that those who attempted to move Jerusalem would also suffer a heavy toll. The phrase 'tear themselves to pieces' (A.V. 'be cut in pieces') is used in Lev. 21:5 in regard to cuttings being made in the flesh in token of mourning. The metaphorical lacerations of Zech. 12:3 would cause mourning and grievous disappointment.

Furthermore, Jehovah declared that He would smite the horses of the attackers with terror and blindness and afflict the riders with insanity. One writer dramatically depicts the scene. 'The terrified horses of the cavalry of the assembled hosts, being thus suddenly smitten with bewilderment or terror, are represented as unable any longer to be guided by bit and bridle. The riders in their madness are described as unable to manage their steeds, while the steeds themselves are portrayed as struck with blindness, and therefore unable to escape from the dangers around them. And while the enemies of God's people will find themselves in such straits at the very moment when they imagined that they had gained the victory and, instead of chasing the vanquished Jews in headlong flight, they themselves are described as rushing upon destruction.' All the power of the enemy will be nullified by the Divine action, and a complete state of panic will be created. Centuries earlier, Deut. 28:28 detailed such an affliction as the judgement of God, and it would perhaps be unwise to discount the picture as entirely metaphorical rather than literal.

At the critical time, Jehovah would 'open His eyes' upon the house of Judah, i.e. He would show favour to Judah (cf. Gen.

44:21). What had happened was for their deliverance. The chieftains (or chiliarchs, i.e. rulers over a thousand) of Judah, with deep conviction, would acknowledge Jerusalem as their bulwark. The city was their stronghold, but the strength of the city was in God.

In startling similes, Jehovah then declared that He would make the chieftains (or chiliarchs) of Judah like a pot of fire among wood and a torch of fire among sheaves, destroying everything on every side. The pot of fire was a chafing pan full of burning coals set among faggots (1 Sam. 2:14) and the torch of fire was literally a flaming torch which would soon set fire to the sheaves of corn and completely devastate everything in sight. In such fashion would Judah's chieftains (and inferentially Judah as a whole) completely destroy the Gentile nations gathered against them.

In consequence of the Divine interposition and the exploits inspired by God, Jerusalem would be inhabited again in its own place. The implication is that the city had been affected by the attacks made upon it and possibly even partially destroyed (see Zech. 14:2). In such a case, the city might be rebuilt on a different site or upon the foundations of the old city, in which case all traces of the damage done would be concealed. It was the latter that was envisaged. Jerusalem would rise again on the same site ('in her own place, even in Jerusalem') and the metropolis would again be fully populated – in part, by some who may have fled before the oncoming forces.

Deliverance would come first to the country-dwellers before it came to Jerusalem, however, since they were relatively defenceless as compared with the occupants of the fortified city. The latter would have no cause for boasting above the people of Judah. Each would have his due share of honour. Perowne (op. cit., p. 131) says that 'the meaning seems to be that the besiegers shall reel back like drunken men from the walls of Jerusalem (v. 2), smitten with panic by God (v. 4); the first to fall upon them and put them to the sword shall be, not the inhabitants of the besieged city by sallying forth from its walls, though they by their gallant and successful defence had rightly been regarded as the bulwark of the whole land (v. 5), but the inhabitants of the open country, who shall have the honour of consuming their adversaries (v. 6), and so of saving themselves and then the capital, which as the result of their prowess shall be completely delivered'. This was, of course, a complete reversal of what would normally happen. In ordinary warfare, the dwellers in the villages and open country suffer first, but in this instance, the city will be besieged and it is the villagers and countrymen who will come to the aid of the beleaguered garrison.

On the other hand, God declared that the inhabitants of Jerusalem in that day, would be under His protection. He would be their shield and no one could, therefore, destroy the city or the population. The feeble weakling (the same word as in 1 Sam. 2:4) would be as valiant as David, the great hero of Jewish history. The house of David in turn would be as God, as the angel of Jehovah. The significance of the angel of Jehovah has already been discussed, and the plain indication is that 'the royal family shall lead the nation no less worthily than the angel of Jehovah did in old time'.

Again, in that day, Jehovah declared that He would seek to destroy all the nations that came against Jerusalem. Rashi renders this last clause of the sub-section, 'I will make research as to destroying them and I will make minute inquiry into their guilt.' There is no suggestion of Divine inability or even of possible change of mind. There was to be a full investigation and the appropriate punishment would be meted out and it would be in proportion to the transgressions committed.

The second sub-section of Zech. 12 relates the effect of the vision of Messiah upon the people.

'And I will pour upon the house of David, and upon the inhabitants of Jerusalem, the spirit of grace and of supplication. And they shall look to me whom they have pierced, and they shall mourn for him, as one mourns for his only son, and shall be in bitterness for him, as one who is in bitterness for his firstborn. In that day shall there be a great mourning in Jerusalem, as the mourning of Hadadrimmon in the valley of Megiddon. And the land shall mourn, every family apart; the family of the house of David apart, and their wives apart; the family of the house of Nathan apart, and their wives apart; the family of the house of Shimei apart, and their wives apart; all the families that remain, every family apart, and their wives apart' (12:10–14).

The miraculous deliverance of Judah and Jerusalem, described in the first nine verses of the chapter, cannot be separated from the repentance and conversion of the people, detailed in the closing verses. Whenever there is a turning to God, however slight the inclination of heart towards Him, God turns in response to the soul's desire. It may perhaps be assumed that the Divine interposition on behalf of the beleaguered city and the invaded country is not unconnected with the spiritual attitude of the people. But their awakening and spiritual revival in the truest and fullest sense can only spring out of their contrition and heartfelt penitence for their sin and particularly for the blackest crime of deicide of which the nation was culpable. The chapter indicates that that will happen coincidentally with a copious spiritual effusion and a revelation of the Messiah who had been pierced.

The 'spirit of grace and of supplication' will be poured out upon the house of David and the inhabitants of Jerusalem, i.e. not merely the effusion of the Holy Spirit promised in Joel 2:28, but the creation by His power of a spiritual attitude in which grace is able to operate and the soul bows down before its Maker. The outpouring occurs first upon the house of David, clearly implying that descendants of the royal line occupy the place of rule and leadership of the nation, but the inhabitants of the city are also the recipients.

The consequence of this work of the Holy Spirit in the individuals is that a revelation is made of the Messiah – 'they shall look to me whom they have pierced'. It has been thought that, in view of the next clause, the word 'me' in the Massoretic text is a scribal error for 'him', but almost all the mss. and versions support the word 'me'. To the Christian, there can be no question as to the identity of the Person thus described: it is obviously the Lord Jesus Christ. Rabbi Solomon Bar Isaac, or Rashi, the Jewish commentator, rendered the clause, 'And they (i.e. the house of David and the inhabitants of Jerusalem) shall look up to Me because of Him whom they (i.e. the nations which come against Jerusalem) have pierced.' Aben Ezra, however, translated it, 'All the heathen shall look to me to see what I shall do to those who pierced Messiah, the son of Joseph.' Abarband says, 'It is more correct to interpret the passage of Messiah, the son of Joseph . . . for he shall be a mighty man of valour of the tribe of Joseph, and shall at first be captain of the Lord's host in that war (namely against Gog and Magog), but in that war shall die.' The rabbis fairly generally apply the passage to Messiah ben Joseph, who was to suffer and die, and not Messiah ben David, who was to reign in power and glory – a distinction invented by themselves. When the revelation of the crucified Messiah is made and the people realize that He is the One whom their forefathers pierced – or delivered up to be crucified – the whole nation will mourn for Him. Then will the language of Isa. 53 become pertinent to those for whom it was primarily intended. The rejection of Christ was a crowning act of contumacy and now they will deem it such for themselves.

As they realize the enormity of their guilt, they will give themselves to mourning unparalleled in the nation's history. The bitterness of remorse and regret will sweep over them as their eyes are opened to a realization of the Person who was crucified at Calvary, and their bitterness will be comparable to that felt by the mourner for an only son. They will lament for Him as for a first-born son. Unger says (op. cit., pp. 215–16), 'Mourning for an only son is represented in the Old Testament as the acme of sorrow that may invade a home (Amos 8:10), and the death-wail over the first-born became proverbial in Israel from the time of the tenth plague in Egypt and the Exodus (Exod. 11:6).'

The mourning in Jerusalem is compared with that of Hadadrimmon in the valley of Megiddo. Hadadrimmon was a city near Jezreel and was the spot at which Josiah was slain by Pharaoh-Necho in 609 B.C. (1 Kings 23:9; 2 Chron. 35:22). 'He was the first king of Judah,' says Smith, 'to fall in battle and leave his country at the mercy of foreign conquerors. His death was a catastrophic loss for Judah, for with him passed away the last bulwark against the flood of wickedness which now swept through the land and carried it to its destruction.' The king was only thirty-nine and the nation's grief was deep and universal. An official decree appointed an annual day of mourning in memory of the event, and the elegies composed on him by Jeremiah were still sung many years after. If the lamentations then were widespread, they were but typical of those in which the nation is yet to indulge.

Every family was to mourn separately and those of David,

Nathan, Levi and Shimei were specifically named, the first two being representative of the royal house and the other two of the priestly tribe. Pusey writes, 'The sorrow shall be universal but also individual, the whole land, and that family by family; the royal family in the direct line of its kings, and in a branch from Nathan, a son of David and whole brother of Solomon (1 Chron 3:5), which was continued on in private life, yet was still to be an ancestral line of Jesus (Luke 3:31); in like way the main priestly family from Levi, and a subordinate line from a grandson of Levi, the family of Shimei (Num. 3:21); and all the remaining families, each with their separate sorrow.' Husbands and wives would mourn separately from each other – an indication of the serious and solemn character of the occasion, sexual intercourse being refrained from at such times (see e.g. Exod. 19:15). Such will be the effect of the revelation of the Messiah as the One whom the nation had pierced.

CHAPTER 20

Israel's Cleansing

The penitential sorrow when Israel sets eyes on the One Who was crucified on their behalf – wounded for their transgressions and bruised for their iniquities (Isa. 53:5) – with the sense of guilt entailed in their awakening, will naturally demand some means of cleansing from sin and defilement. This is the subject of the next section of the prophecy.

'In that day there shall be a fountain opened to the house of David and to the inhabitants of Jerusalem for sin and for uncleanness. And it shall come to pass in that day, says Jehovah of hosts, that I will cut off the names of the idols out of the land, and they shall no more be remembered. And also I will cause the prophets and the unclean spirit to pass out of the land' (13:1, 2).

The opening words of this sub-section at once indicate that the events described all fall within the period already referred to in the previous chapter, i.e. the day of Jehovah. The many references to that period portray it as one of clouds and thick darkness, when the indignation of Jehovah will result in the meting out of punishment upon a guilty world, and Israel will experience the unparalleled suffering and trial of the great tribulation (Joel 1:15; 2:1, 2; 3:16; Isa. 2:10–18; 34:1–8; Jer. 30:7, etc). That period will, of course conclude with the Second Advent of Christ. But if Israel is to enter into the blessings of His kingdom, her people will need cleansing to render them suitable to be subjects of it. So the prophet declared that a fountain for sin and uncleanness would be opened. The word 'fountain' is never used of a stagnant pool and it implies a spring of fresh water. It was to wash away the defilement of the people, as the red heifer was provided for their purification in an earlier day (Num. 19). That fountain could, of course, be nothing else than Calvary and the cleansing which became available through the blood out-poured then.

It was provided for the house of David and for the inhabitants of Jerusalem. The royal family were the shepherds or rulers of Israel and it was imperative that the defilement which hindered their communion with God should be removed, in order that they might be fit to shepherd His people. 'Sin and uncleanness' were terms used for idolatry (1 Kings 17:30; Ezek. 7:19, 20), but they doubtless covered the actual condition of the nation as well as the spiritual state.

The besetting sin of Israel in earlier days (but apparently not in the post-exilic period) was that of idolatry and for this they were Divinely chastised on a number of occasions. But now God declared that He would cut off the name of the idols and that they would be remembered no more. 'The name of the idol', says Barnes (op. cit., p. 96) 'represents the idol as a power which exercises influence over its worshippers and induces them to pay it reverence and ascribe supernatural works to it. To "cut off the names of the idols" is to take away all their authority and all men's acknowledgement of them. Men will cease to invoke them.' The idols would no more be remembered. In other words there was to be a complete extinction of idolatry. There are indications in the New Testament that idolatry will affect the nation again in a future day (Rev. 9:20; 13:4, 15). It is clear, therefore, that the pledge in Zech. 13:2 has not yet been implemented. Idolatry and false prophecy were obviously intended as typical of all forms of spiritual impurity or unfaithfulness: restoration to communion with God was patently dependent upon their extirpation. It has been maintained by some that the references to idolatry indicate that this part of the prophecy was uttered in pre-exilic days, because idolatry was not in evidence in the post-exilic period. But this ignores the Biblical practice of using the occurrences of the past as the basis of warnings for the future.

The prophets and the unclean spirit were also to be dismissed from the land. The association of the two indicates that the prophets in question were false ones. Chambers (op. cit., p. 100) argues that the spirit of uncleanness is 'not merely a pervading principle, but an active, conscious agency, standing in direct contrast with the Spirit of grace (12:10), which works in its human instruments and leads them to their lying utterances. The false prophet, as well as the true, were subject to an influence from without (cf. 1 Kings 22:21–23; Rev. 16:14; 2

Thess. 2:9; 10; 1 Tim. 4:2).' Both land and people were to be cleansed.

The subject of the false prophet was still pursued in the next few verses.

'And it shall come to pass, that when any shall yet prophesy, then his father and his mother who begot him shall say to him, You shall not live; for you speak lies in the name of Jehovah. And his father and his mother who begot him shall thrust him through when he prophesies. And it shall come to pass in that day, that the prophets shall be ashamed every one of his vision, when he prophesies: neither shall they wear a hairy mantle to deceive. But he shall say, I am no prophet, I am a husbandman; for a churl possessed me as a serf from my youth. And one shall say to him, What are these wounds between your hands? Then he shall answer, Those with which I was wounded in the house of my friends' (13:3–6).

Despite the banishment from the land of false prophecy and uncleanness, there will apparently be individuals who will still have the impudence to prophesy without a divine commission or authority. Centuries earlier, specific instructions had been given for such a case – 'the prophet, who shall presume to speak a word in my name, which I have not commanded him to speak, or that shall speak in the name of other gods, even that prophet shall die' (Deut. 18:20; 13:6). Accordingly, Jehovah required his parents to be responsible to inflict on him the prescribed penalty of death. Obedience to God took priority even over parental affection. Because their apostate son had told lies in the name of Jehovah, he was not to be allowed to live. His own parents were obliged to pronounce his sentence and to stab the renegade to death. The words are not irrelevant to the present day. Our Lord foretold that, prior to His second advent, false prophets would arise (Matt. 24:24). There can be no toleration of such. God's honour is at stake.

The jeopardy in which the false prophet stands and the conviction of his own conscience will evidently cause him to disavow entirely all claims to the possession of the prophetic gift. Shame and fear will compel him to dissemble. He will discard the hairy mantle which he formerly wore and will deny all connection with the prophetic office. 'The hairy mantle worn by the prophets (2 Kings 1:8) was not a form of ascetic discipline, but a symbol of the prophet's grief for the sins which he was commissioned to reprove. It was an acted parable of repentance.' It originated with Elijah, but in time became the badge of the prophet. Even in New Testament days, it was worn by John the Baptist (Mk. 1:6). But, in the day of which Zechariah spoke, it will be dangerous for a deceiver to wear the prophetic garb without the authority to utter God's message to the people.

Such a man will furthermore vehemently disclaim even having occupied the prophetic office, using the untrue argument that he had been sold as a slave in his youth, whose time belonged entirely to his master. He will declare that he had been only a tiller of the ground and one who was obviously so tied to his owner and his work that it would have been impossible for him to engage in a ministry which would necessitate complete freedom to travel wherever he was directed by the Spirit of God. There may also be a hint that, in such a lowly state of serfdom, he was unlikely to acquire the knowledge or ability required by a prophet.

His dissimulation will not deceive everyone, however. Working in the fields and stripped to the waist, he will be unable to hide the scars on his breast, and those who are dissatisfied with his explanations will demand to know the meaning of these wounds. *Prima facie*, they seem the self-inflicted wounds of a worshipper of the false gods, and caused by a sense of guilt and the impression that the punishment of the body would propitiate the gods (1 Kings 18:28). The injuries could not have been caused by his owner: the scars borne by a slave would be in the back and not in the front. What explanation can he give? Kimchi writes, 'He shall say these wounds are not on account of prophecy, but my friends wounded and chastised me because I was abandoned, and was not industrious in cultivating the land in my youth: and they beat me that I should cease from the profligacy of young men, and should set to my work. And the reason for the wounds being in the hands is that they used to bind his hands and feet that he should not go out.' While this is a possible interpretation of his words, it is more likely that he alleges that the injuries were received in a drunken brawl in the house of some of his dissolute friends. This would add emphasis to his claim of unsuitability to be a prophet. Verse 6 is sometimes interpreted as applying to Messiah, but it is more logical to regard it as part of the preceding sub-section and not of the following one. The question was clearly asked of the one who is the subject of the earlier verses and not of another to whom reference is not made until the following verse. For no obvious reason, except the committee's apparent preference and mistaken impression of relevance, the N.E.B. transposes these verses to follow Zech. 11:17. There seems no textual justification for this. In fact, as Cowles points out (*The Minor Prophets*, p. 367), 'The close analogy between the false prophet, whose hands had been gashed and pierced "in the house of his friends", and the Messiah, whose hands were pierced in a deathly crucifixion among those who ought to have been His friends' shows how appropriate the verses are to this particular chapter.

The last three verses of Zech. 13 are plainly concerned with the Messiah as the shepherd and the nation as His sheep.

'Awake, O sword, against my shepherd, and against the man that is my fellow, says Jehovah of hosts. Smite the shepherd, and the sheep shall be scattered: and I will turn my hand upon the little ones. And it shall come to pass that in all the land, says Jehovah, two parts therein shall be cut off and die; but the third shall be left therein. And I will bring the third part through the fire, and will refine them as silver is refined, and will try them as gold is tried. They shall call on my name, and I will answer them. I will say, He is my people: and he shall say, Jehovah is my God (13:7–9).

In Zech. 11 the foolish shepherd had been contrasted with the good shepherd. In the closing verses of Zech. 13 the true prophet is contrasted with the false prophet and the manner of his wounding with the self-inflicted scars of the latter. Once again too he is introduced in the character of the shepherd. The change of subject is not so abrupt and dramatic as, superficially, it might appear. Expositors have varied in their identification of this One, and it has been suggested that Judas Maccabeus, Pekah, Jehoiakim, and others were the one here represented. But there can be no dubiety on this matter, for our Lord quoted Zech. 13:7 just prior to His betrayal and applied the words to Himself and His disciples (Matt. 26:31; Mark 14:27). His quotation was from the Septuagint except that He used the future tense.

Jehovah Himself called upon the sword to awake as though the weapon was a living thing (cf. Jer. 47:6). The sword was the expressive symbol of judicial power. The highest order of governor in the Roman provinces was the one in whom the 'right of the sword', *jus gladii*, or the power of life and death was vested (Rom. 13:4). The One who apostrophized the sword was the One with the supreme authority, and He summoned the sword into activity. The implication, of course, was that death was about to be judicially inflicted (cf. Ps. 17:13). But the One who was to be executed was described as God's shepherd (John 10:14) and 'the man that is my fellow'. Our Lord's citation of the verse leaves no room for doubt that the One thus described was Himself and that it was His death that was in view. That death was, in fact, essential if the fountain for sin and uncleanness, of which verse 1 spoke, was to be opened. Cleansing could only be effected because of the blood shed at Calvary. His death was a judicial one. He bore the penalty of the law. But His was a vicarious death, merited by the sheep and borne by the shepherd.

Not only was He God's shepherd, but His fellow. The N.E.B. renders this (quite unjustifiably) as 'him who works with me' and thereby, of course, eliminates the evidence of our Lord's equality with God. The word *anith* is used eleven times in the Book of Leviticus and its significance is the nearest kin. Hengstenberg renders the phrase 'A man, my nearest relation' and rationalistic De Wette as 'the man my equal'. One writer puts it succinctly when he says that the idea of the nearest one involves 'community of physical or spiritual descent, according to which he whom God calls His neighbour cannot be a mere man, but can only be one who participates in the Divine nature, or is essentially Divine. The Shepherd of Jehovah, whom the sword is to smite, is therefore, no other than the Messiah, who is also identified with Jehovah in Zech. 12:10; or the Good Shepherd, who says of Himself, "I and My Father are one" (John 10:30)'. The N.E.B. rendering could well be viewed in the light of Moore's comment (op. cit., p. 213) that the word *anith* is never used to indicate similarity of office, as Socinians assert on this passage, but always nearness of relation or kindred. Hence it here must refer to a human relation to Jehovah, which, of course, must be a divine nature. Hence we have here clearly a twofold nature in the suffering Messiah, human and divine.' It was this One who was to be smitten with the sword.

The result of the smiting of the Shepherd was that the sheep would be scattered, and the New Testament record shows how literally and quickly the words were fulfilled in the case of our Lord's disciples (Matt. 26:31, 56). The prophecy extended beyond the immediate desertion of the disciples, however, and patently predicted the worldwide dispersion of the Jewish race, a flock without a shepherd. The past nineteen centuries of Israel's *diaspora* have carried prophecy into history. Not only would the sheep in general be scattered, but God would also turn His 'hand upon the little ones'. The expression is consistently used in a punitive and uncomforting sense and does not, as is suggested by some, imply mercy to the faithful ones. Indeed our Lord plainly warned His disciples that persecution, suffering and death would be their portion (Matt. 24:9; John 15:20, etc). A comparison with Zech. 11:7, 11 might have saved the N.E.B. from the absurd translation of 'little ones' as 'shepherd boys'.

Jehovah then declared that, in all the land, two-thirds would be cut off and die, and one-third be left. Hengstenberg has an interesting comment on this verse. He says, 'The whole of the Jewish nation is introduced here as an inheritance left by the Shepherd who has been put to death, which inheritance is divided into three parts: death claiming the privilege of the first-born, and so receiving two portions, and life one – a division similar to that which David made in the case of the Moabites (2 Sam. 8:2).' Most commentators apply this verse to the Jewish war of A.D. 67 – 70, when a million and a half Jews perished by sword, famine and pestilence, and thousands were sold as slaves. But as Perowne points out, those who survived were not a refined and regenerated people, but unbelievers. It seems more probable, therefore, that the prophecy looks on to the sufferings of the great tribulation and to the preservation of a faithful remnant in that day (Rev. 7:1–8; 14:1–5).

This is confirmed by the concluding verse of the chapter, where it is stated that the third who remain will be brought into the fire and refined as silver is refined and tried as gold is tried. The intense heat of the furnace of the tribulation through which the future saints pass will purge all the dross and remove all the impurities and they will finally emerge freed from all that might hinder their suitability to enter into the millennial kingdom. In the midst of the fire, the suffering remnant will call on the name of Jehovah – a prayer born out of adversity but patently leading to repentance and regeneration, for He will not only hear but answer their cry. The reply from heaven regards the whole of the remnant as one person, 'He is my people,' and the people gladly respond, 'Jehovah is my God' (cf. Jer. 32:28; Ezek. 37:23). The centuries of suffering and the fires of tribulation past, they will be established in blessing in their own land under the beneficent rule of their Messiah.

CHAPTER 21

The Second Advent

Zech. 14 arises naturally out of the last three verses of the previous chapter and in some respects it may be regarded as an expansion and extension of the subject of those verses, 'attention being concentrated, however', as Perowne remarks (op. cit., p. 141), 'on the city rather than on the land (13:8), and on the final act rather than on the long previous process of purifying discipline'. The chapter is wholly prophetic and none of the events described therein has yet been fulfilled. It is interpreted by many works as a description of the current and future experience of the Church, but this interpretation is clearly inappropriate. The only satisfactory interpretation is that which regards the prophecy as literal. As Feinberg (*God Remembers*, pp. 248–249) says, if this passage 'is interpreted in the literal sense, it harmonizes with all that Zechariah has revealed thus far and with the prophecies concerning the consummation for Israel found throughout the Scripture.'

The chapter opens with a description of Jerusalem's suffering in the day of trouble looming ahead.

'Behold a day comes to Jehovah, when your spoil shall be divided in the midst of you. For I will gather all nations against Jerusalem to battle; and the city shall be taken, and the houses rifled and the women raped. And half of the city shall go forth into captivity, but the residue of people shall not be cut off from the city' (14:1, 2).

The period described is obviously the day of Jehovah, so frequently referred to in the Old Testament prophets, although the expression used in verse 1 is not the usual one in this connection. The phrase is literally, 'A day is coming – Jehovah's'. The events detailed in the chapter are those which are to occur during the period of judgement of the day of Jehovah and leave no doubt as to the significance of the phrase. The dire straits to which Jerusalem has been reduced are evident from the first verse. The city has been so completely subjugated by the armies which attacked her that the soldiers are able unhinderedly to apportion between themselves the booty they have taken as they have rampaged through the streets. Houses rifled and shops presumably looted, everything of value has been pillaged.

According to Zechariah, all nations will be gathered against Jerusalem (cf. Ezek. 38 and 39). From all directions, forces will pour into the land. Invaders from Egypt clashing with hordes from the north (Dan. 11:40), western armies intervening to implement their pledge of protection (Dan. 9:27), eastern multitudes pouring in from another direction (Rev. 16:12), all acting in pursuance of their own aims and objects, will be unaware that another hand controls their activities and directs their course that they might be prepared for their own destruction. But judgement is first to fall upon God's own people and the nations are employed as His instrument for the purpose.

The statement of Zech. 1:15 seems applicable in this instance also – the nations exceeded their commission and added to the sufferings of Israel. Following the investiture of the city, every house will apparently be invaded by the rude soldiery and all the horrors of war enacted in rape, cruelty and murder. Half of the population will be carried away captive, doubtless to fill the labour camps of the enemy or to satisfy the lust of the troops. Only a small number will be left in the city, a remnant who are not cut off. The sufferings and tribulations of the centuries will seem to have no end. Yet, at the moment of the people's greatest extremity, salvation comes.

'Then shall Jehovah go forth and fight against those nations as when He fought in the day of battle. And His feet shall stand in that day on the mount of Olives, which is before Jerusalem on the east, and the mount of Olives shall cleave in its middle toward the east and toward the west, and there shall be a very great valley. And half of the mountain shall recede toward the north, and half of it toward the south. And you shall flee by the valley of my mountains; for the valley of the mountains shall reach unto Azal: yes, you shall flee, like as you fled from before the earthquake in the days of Uzziah king of Judah: and Jehovah my God shall come and all the holy ones with you' (14:3–5).

The small remnant left in the city might well despair: despite all the promises of the past, their future could only be total extinction. It is at this point that Jehovah will suddenly intervene, breaking into man's world in all His power as a mighty warrior (Judg. 4:14; Ps. 108:11) and accompanied by all the 'holy ones', i.e. both the angels and the redeemed (Jude 14). In the past He has on more than one occasion fought for His people (e.g. Josh. 10:14) and now He will do so again. The tremendous forces of the nations will evidently smash the army of Israel and, in a virulent and venomous display of antisemitism, use the utmost brutality and sadism in their treatment of the chosen race, but God's purposes can never be thwarted and when He comes, it will be in incomparable might to crush and destroy His foes and to deliver His people.

Olivet, which saw the ascent of our Lord Jesus Christ, is to be the scene of His return (for Jehovah's revelation of Himself must surely be in the person of the Messiah). It was from this mountain that the shekinah glory departed prior to the Babylonian captivity (Ezek. 11:23) and it will be from this direction that it will reappear in a future day (Ezek. 43:2). 'The mount of Olives,' says Pusey, 'is the central eminence of a line of hills, of rather more than a mile in length, overhanging the city, from which it is separated only by the narrow bed of the valley of the brook of Kidron. It rises 187 ft above mount Zion, 295 ft above mount Moriah, 443 ft. above Gethsemane, and lies between the city and the wilderness toward the Dead Sea.' At its highest point, it is 2,680 ft above sea-level. When the Lord's feet stand on Olivet, the prophet predicted that the mountain will split apart, one part moving northward and the other part southward, so that a great valley will be formed. There was an earthquake on July 11th, 1927, which shook Palestine from the Sea of Galilee to the border of Egypt and, after the tremors, geologists discovered a fault in Olivet, running from east to west. Prof. Bailey Willis, of Stanford University, said that the land could expect to suffer from seismological disturbances and that the area around Jerusalem was a region of potential danger, a fault line, along which earth slippage might occur, passing directly under the Mount of Olives. It is evident, therefore, that what Zechariah described is precisely what geologists would expect to occur. The alteration in the physical contour of the country will leave Jerusalem standing on a mountain in the centre of a very large valley (cf. Ps. 48:1–3).

Mabie says, 'This earthquake will not only change the whole topography of Palestine, but it will cut in two the mountain backbone of that land, right through the Mount of Olives. By it at one stroke, east and west, the land will divide, and a great ship canal be formed from the Mediterranean Sea to the Jordan valley and the Dead Sea. The waters of the great sea, rushing down through that earthquake chasm, with a fall about eight times the height of Niagara – or an average of about 22 ft. to the mile – would fill the Jordan valley to the sea of Galilee and above. To the southward the waters would sweep down to the Gulf of Aqaba and the Red Sea. So, if the Jordan valley should remain at about its present level, it would form the bed of a great and deep inland sea, approaching to the very suburbs of Jerusalem. So the city of the great king would become the seaport of the world – the business emporium of the nations.' The commercial potentialities are patent.

The cataclysmic earthquake will provide the solution to the problem of the beleaguered remnant in Jerusalem. The newly-formed valley will extend from Azal (the location of which is uncertain) across the Kidron valley to the wall of the city, providing a way of escape from Jerusalem, which the refugees will gladly take. It is said that the people will flee as they fled from before the earthquake in the days of Uzziah. No details are given in the Biblical record of that earlier earthquake, but two centuries before Zechariah, Amos stated that he began to prophesy in the days of Uzziah, 'two years before the earthquake' (Amos 1:1). The earlier prophet also predicted that Jehovah would 'roar out of Zion and utter His voice from Jerusalem' (Amos 1:2). Subsequently (presumably after the earthquake had taken place), he declared that 'the lion has roared' and 'the Lord God has spoken' (Amos 3:8). His prophecy gave no indication of the date of the earthquake nor any further details concerning it (except possibly those in Amos 8:8; 9:5), although C. T. Francisco, in *Introducing the Old Testament,* argues that Amos 4:13 associates the earthquake with a total eclipse of the sun, which is known to have occurred during Uzziah's reign.

It is evident from the words of Amos that the earthquake was regarded as a Divine judgement and that it was apparently accompanied by thunder and lightning, the roll of thunder and the rumble of the trembling earth being identified with the roar of Jehovah and the sound of His voice. It is equally clear from Zechariah that this seismic disturbance was of such a character, either in its context or its effects, as to live permanently in the memory of the people, and to be a fitting comparison for the terrible upheaval and topographical changes occurring at the Second Advent. But when did it take place and what were the circumstances in which it happened?

The historical record discloses that when Uzziah 'was strong, his heart was lifted up to his destruction' and that he entered the temple to burn incense on the golden altar. The king resisted the priests who attempted to prevent his sacrilegious act, but God intervened and, as leprosy rose in Uzziah's forehead, the priests thrust him out of the temple (2 Chron. 26:16–21). Josephus states that, at the time of Uzziah's impious attempt, the earth quaked and the voice of God was heard (*Ant.* ix 10:4) and, according to tradition, the inhabitants of the city fled in terror from the place. If this is correct the earthquake, which caused such consternation at the time and which was still remembered so long afterwards, was due to the interposition of God, and marked His judgement of the guilty king. The fear caused by the enemy and by the earthquake and its serious effects in Zechariah's day will drive the inhabitants of Jerusalem once again to flee in terror and this time along the new valley.

Other phenomena of this period of judgement are described in the succeeding verses.

'And it shall come to pass in that day that there shall not be light, the bright ones shall be contracted: but it shall be an unique day, which is known to Jehovah, not day nor night: but it shall come to pass that, at evening time, there shall be light. And it shall come to pass in that day, that living waters shall go out from Jerusalem; half of them toward the eastern sea, and half of them toward the western sea; in summer and in winter shall it be. And Jehovah shall be king over all the earth; in that day Jehovah shall be one and his name one. All the land shall be transformed like the Arabah from Geba to Rimmon south of Jerusalem: and she shall be lifted up and shall dwell in her place, from Benjamin's gate to the place of the first gate, to the corner gate, and from the tower of Hananeel to the king's winepresses. And men shall dwell in it, and there shall be no more curse; but Jerusalem shall dwell safely' (14:6–11).

Unger renders verse 6, 'And it shall be in that day that there shall not be the light of the luminaries but thick murkiness.' In

His Olivet discourse, our Lord predicted signs in the heavens at the time of the Second Advent (Matt. 24:29, 30). According to Zechariah, at the time of the Lord's return to earth, not only will there be seismological disturbances, but the heavenly bodies will fail to give their light, and the earth will be in a state of mingled light and darkness. Barnes (op. cit., p. 102) puts it aptly 'for a small space chaos is to return and light, the first-born of the cosmos will fail. Darkness, partial or complete, is sometimes the accompaniment of earthquakes.' It will be an unique day, known or understood only by Jehovah. It will be neither day nor night, but at evening time light will be restored.

The upheaval caused by the earthquake will leave Jerusalem as a kind of watershed and perennial streams will flow from the city to the east and to the west to irrigate the thirsty land which has needed water for all the centuries. Joel 3:18 foretells a similar transformation at the same time. Unger considers that the convulsion of the earth at the Lord's coming will open up vast subterranean springs and that the new rivers will flow to the Dead Sea on the one side and to the Mediterranean on the other. Most rivers and streams in Palestine today are seasonal and dry up in the summer. But these springs are to be permanent and they will flow in summer as well as in winter, bringing blessing to land and people. Water is one of the greatest needs of this region, and the provision of an abundant supply will be deemed a boon that must have originated in some supernatural action. It will, of course, be through the presence of Christ alone that this and every other blessing comes – in that day as in this.

In that day Jehovah is to be acknowledged as king by the whole earth. Naturally, His reign will not be restricted to earth for the whole of God's creation is going to be placed under the headship of Christ, and every being in the heights above or in the depths beneath will be compelled to acknowledge His sovereignty. Many of the heathen gods were worshipped under more than one name, their character being revealed by their names. In that day, however, Jehovah alone will be worshipped. He will be one and His name one. The full revelation of Himself is unambiguously made in that one name.

The whole land is to be transformed in topography and become like a plain, stretching from Geba to Rimmon, and Jerusalem alone will be left in a position of pre-eminence. According to the prophet, the plain is to be like Arabah. Chambers (op. cit., p. 111) says, 'The article is emphatic in "the plain", which in Hebrew always denotes the Arabah or Ghor, the largest and most celebrated of all the plains of Judea, the great valley extending from Lebanon to the farther side of the Dead Sea. Geba was on the northern frontier of Judah (cf. 2 Kings 23:8). Rimmon, distinguished from two other Rimmons on the north (Josh. 19:13; Judg. 20:45), by the added clause, 'south of Jerusalem,' was a city on the border of Edom, given up by Judah to the Simeonites (Josh. 15:32; 19:7). In consequence of this depression of all the surrounding country, Jerusalem becomes high. The capital, seated on her hills, shines conspicuous as the only elevation in a very wide region.'

The exalted metropolis was to be peacefully inhabited, the occupied area being delineated as from Benjamin's gate (or the gate of Ephraim – 2 Kings 14:13) to the centre of the north wall, through which the road ran to Benjamin and Ephraim; it was to reach from there to the first gate to its east in the north-east corner of the city (possibly identical with the 'old gate'); from thence it extended to the corner gate in the north-western extremity of the city (2 Kings 14:13; Jer. 31:38); then from the tower of Hananeel in the north-west corner of the temple area, it stretched southwards to the king's winepresses near the valley of Hinnom. It was to be fully populated and people would live there in security and no more danger would threaten.

Verses 12 to 15 really supplement verses 1 to 3 and disclose how the foes of the Jerusalem remnant are destroyed.

'And this shall be the plague with which Jehovah will smite all the peoples who have fought against Jerusalem. Their flesh shall consume away while they stand on their feet, and their eyes shall consume away in their sockets, and their tongue shall consume away in their mouth. And it shall come to pass in that day that a great tumult from Jehovah shall be among them, and they shall lay hold every one on the hand of his neighbour, and his hand shall rise up against the hand of his neighbour. And Judah also shall fight at Jerusalem: and the wealth of all the nations round about shall be gathered together, gold and silver and apparel in great abundance. And so shall be the plague of the horse, of the mule, of the camel, and of the ass, and of all the beasts that shall be in these camps, as this plague' (14:12–15).

The three means by which comes destruction of the enemies of God's people are stated in these verses to be a terrible plague which Jehovah inflicts upon them, a panic with which He confuses them, and the intrepid valour of the people of Judah. Behind all three media is clearly the person of Jehovah Himself, and the victory belongs not to man but to Him.

An unparalleled plague was to smite the great armies which were arrayed against Jerusalem and which so brutally and ruthlessly maltreated its inhabitants. They had engaged in military combat, not against Judah but, by implication, against God, and their flesh would inexplicably fester where they stood. They had looked covetously on Jerusalem's possessions, and their eyes would rot away in their sockets. They had impudently spoken against God and His people, and their tongues would become putrid in their mouths. The imagery is appalling: these wretches are doomed to a living death. The plague will come upon them in the moment of their victory. In his book, *In the Days to Come*, W. A. Peterson writes, 'In Hiroshima on August 6th 1945, 60,000 people were killed and 100,000 wounded by one atomic bomb. The flesh literally roasted and fell off the bones of the people who were walking in the streets. In every case the eyes just disappeared, dissolving out on to the cheeks. Apparently the eyes are very sensitive to radiation, and in many cases the tongue as well was loosened and affected.' What man-made weapons are capable of doing is not comparable with what may result from the hand of God, and it is unwise to regard the language used as anything but literal. Verse 15 indicates that the plague will not be confined to human beings but, as would be expected, will affect every beast in the camps of the nations who have gathered against Jerusalem. This is in full accord with Scriptural precedent and the Divine methods (Josh. 6:21).

In addition, a great tumult or consternation, inspired by God, will cause a frightening confusion among the mighty forces. Its nature is not stated, but its result will be a panic-stricken commotion, which causes every man to attack his neighbour and effect a complete mutual annihilation. If the terrifying plague is caused by the emission of rays resulting from some form of thermonuclear explosion, the latter would presumably be accompanied by a tremendous noise which would itself have disastrous effects. Uncontrolled noise can cause emotional instability, disorganized behaviour and violence, and it is not inconceivable that this may be the cause of the mutual antagonism and destruction.

Thirdly it is stated that Judah will fight at Jerusalem. The old rivalry between Judah and Jerusalem now banished, the people's only desire will be to deliver the city. Amid the disarray and confusion resulting from the miraculous interposition of Jehovah, Judah will gallantly rally to the attack. The immense booty captured from the invaders will fall to Judah. Gold, silver, garments, evidently in tremendous quantities, will be taken from the defeated armies, together presumably with all of which they had robbed the population of Jerusalem. The defeat will be conclusive.

CHAPTER 22

Worship and Holiness

Every foe defeated, the Messiah will be supreme and His long-promised reign will ensue. In the Annunciation, Gabriel declared that Mary's Babe would receive 'the throne of his father David' and would 'reign over the house of Jacob for ever' (Luke 1:32, 33). The pledge of the centuries will now be redeemed and our Lord Jesus Christ will reign over the earth. His rule, beneficent although it will be, is to be with a rod of iron, and the nations will be compelled to render obedience to him. Annually they will pay their worship to Him at Jerusalem.

'And it shall come to pass that every one that is left of all the nations which came against Jerusalem shall go up from year to year to worship the King, Jehovah of hosts, and to keep the feast of tabernacles. And it shall be that whoso of all the families of the earth will not come up to Jerusalem to worship the King, Jehovah of hosts, upon them there shall be no rain. And if the family of Egypt go not up and come not, neither shall it be upon them. There shall be the plague, wherewith Jehovah will smite the nations that come not up to keep the feast of tabernacles. This shall be the sin of Egypt and the sin of all the nations that come not up to keep the feast of tabernacles' (14:16–19).

The survivors from the nations who attacked Jerusalem, in many cases, will apparently have turned in repentance to God to learn His righteousness and ways (Isa. 26:9), but all the nations will be required annually to go up to Jerusalem to worship Jehovah the King. Presumably this will be by delegates or representatives, since it is impossible to imagine millions of people making their way to the holy City simultaneously. The occasion of the gathering is the feast of tabernacles. This was held in the seventh month and the rainy season commenced soon afterwards. Perowne suggests that there are three reasons for the choice of this particular festival from the Jewish calendar, viz., (1) the feast of tabernacles was held in the autumn, when travelling would be most convenient and possibly least arduous; (2) it was a festival of thanksgiving for the fruits of the earth, in which all could readily take part; (3) it was the last and greatest festival of the Jewish year, gathering up in itself the year's worship and, at the same time, typifying the ingathering of the nation.

Tabernacles was a seven-day feast of joy and gladness. The people lived for that week in rudely constructed booths, made of tree branches. Unger (op. cit., pp. 265–6) suggests that the reason for the continued observance of this feast during the millennium is that 'it is the only one of the seven feasts of the Lord which at that time will be unfulfilled typically and the only one which will be in process of fulfilment by the kingdom itself. The passover (Lev. 23:4, 5) was fulfilled in the death of Christ the Redeemer (1 Cor. 5:7; 1 Pet. 1:19). The feast of unleavened bread (Lev. 23:6–8) is being fulfilled in the holy, separate walk of the believer in fellowship with his Saviour (1 Cor. 5:6–8; 2 Cor. 7:1; Gal. 5:7–9). The feast of first-fruits (Lev. 23:9–14) was fulfilled in the resurrection of Christ (1 Cor. 15:23. The feast of Pentecost (Lev. 23:15–22) was fulfilled in the formation of the Church at Pentecost fifty days subsequent to the resurrection of Christ (1 Cor. 10:16; 12:12, 13). The feast of trumpets (Lev. 23:23–25) will be fulfilled in the future regathering of Israel at the beginning of the kingdom (Isa. 18:3, 7; 27:12, 13; Ezek. 37:1–14). The day of atonement (Lev. 23:26–32) in its prophetic feature will be fulfilled in the conversion of Israel at the second advent (Zech. 12:10–13; 13:1) and preparatory to the millennium. Only the feast of tabernacles at that time will be unfulfilled in its prophetic aspect as typical of the kingdom rest of Israel after her regathering, and the blessedness typified by that festival will be in process of fulfilment throughout the kingdom age.'

Those who fail to fulfil their obligation of visiting Jerusalem for this feast are to suffer the penalty for their failure – there will be no rainfall in their area. Rain is essential for the land and for the well-being of man. Without it, particularly in hot countries, there would be no harvest, and famine would ensue. It is the sign of God's blessing, and its lack is a serious one. With the Son of God upon the throne of the universe, there can, of course, be no difficulty about the deprivation of one country and the blessing of an adjoining country in this respect.

Egypt, the ancient foe of Israel, is singled out for special mention. Egypt enjoys no rainfall, except in negligible quantities at the coast, and it might be argued that such a penalty would be irrelevant to her. But the ultimate penalty was not merely the withholding of rain, but the famines which inevitably resulted from drought. The fertility of Egypt depends on the annual inundation of the Nile and this is caused by the torrential rains in the region of the Upper Nile. If the rain is withheld in the upper regions of the river, the delta and the river area of Egypt must inevitably suffer. The punishment is, therefore, equally pertinent to Egypt.

The One who sits on the throne will exercise an iron rule. His administration will be just and equitable, but wrongdoing will be punished immediately. His holiness is to characterize not only His actions in general, but even the city of the great King.

'In that day, shall there be on the bells of the horses "Holy to Jehovah", and the pots in Jehovah's house shall be like the bowls before the altar. Yes, every pot in Jerusalem and in Judah shall be holy to Jehovah of hosts; and all who sacrifice shall come and take of them and boil in them. And in that day there shall be no more a Canaanite in the house of Jehovah of hosts' (14:20, 12).

The character of the great Ruler will be reflected in everything about Him. The unclean is to be banished! sin is to be crushed and the evildoer removed. The whole land is to be sanctified to God, but the city of Jerusalem is to be demonstrably set apart to Him. Even the most ordinary things of everyday life are to be holy. On the mitre of Israel's high priest was a golden plate bearing the words, 'Holy to Jehovah'. Even the bells of the horses in that future day will bear the same inscription.

The very domestic utensils in the home are to be sanctified: everything is to be holy to God. The cauldrons used in the temple to boil the flesh of the sacrificial victims before it was eaten were now to become as holy as the sacred bowls in which the blood of the sacrifice was caught to be sprinkled upon the corners of the altar. Where the Messiah ruled, everything became sacred.

There is a practical import for the believer still. The one who belongs to Christ is set apart to Him and that sanctification or separation applies to his whole being and to every sphere of life. The Christian cannot speak of his time, his possessions, his abilities, his wealth. All he has is sanctified to his Lord.

The concluding statement of the book is in harmony with the preceding verses. In a holy city and a holy temple, there is no place for the unholy, and the prophecy declared that in that day, there shall be no Canaanite in the temple. The gross immorality of the Canaanites and the degrading and licentious character of their religion are fairly clearly indicated in the Old Testament record. It was because of their degeneracy, and the danger of Israel's corruption through contact with them, that they were to be extirpated when the land of Canaan was conquered. The term Canaanite was proverbial for a morally unclean person. It also became a metaphor for the trafficker (Hos.11:7, where 'merchant' should read 'Canaan'). It seems incredible that one of such a character should be found in the temple, but now they were to be permanently excluded. Let the Christian also jealously guard his life that no unclean or undesirable thought or action may find a place in it.

So the prophecy concludes with the glorious picture of millennial bliss and holiness. Zechariah does not see beyond the age to come and no glimpse was given to him of the eternal state. Nevertheless, he confirms the statements and predictions of the earlier prophets that an age is to come when evil shall be under rigid restraint and God shall reign supreme in His creation.

Bibliography

J. ADAMS. *The Man Among the Myrtles.* (Charles Scribner's Sons, New York, 1913.)

W. E. BARNES. *Haggai and Zechariah.* (Cambridge University Press, Cambridge, 1917.)

D. BARON. *The Servant of Jehovah.* (Marshall, Morgan & Scott Ltd., London 1954.)

The Visions and Prophecies of Zechariah. (H.C.T.I., London, 1951.)

R. BLAYNEY. *A New Translation of the Prophecies of Zechariah.* (London, 1797.)

J. CALVIN. *Commentary on the Twelve Minor Prophets.* (Banner of Truth Trust, London, n.d.)

T. W. CHAMBERS. 'Zechariah' in *The Minor Prophets*, by J. P. Lange. (Zondervan Publishing House, Grand Rapids, n.d.)

G. N. M. COLLINS. 'Zechariah' in *New Bible Commentary.* (Inter Varsity Press, London, 1953.)

S. R. DRIVER. *The Minor Prophets.*

C. L. FEINBERG. *God Remembers.* (Van Kampen Press, Wheaton, 1950.)

A. C. GAEBELEIN. *Studies in Zechariah.* (Francis E. Fitch, New York, 1911.)

H. GRATTAN GUINNESS. *Light for the Last Days.* (Marshall, Morgan & Scott Ltd., London, 1917.)

G. G. HACKMAN. *The Book of Zechariah.* (Muhlenberg Press, Philadelphia, 1948.)

D. E. HART-DAVIES. *The Severity of God* (Pickering & Inglis Ltd., Glasgow. n.d)

H. A. IRONSIDE. *The Minor Prophets.* (Loizeaux Brothers, New York, n.d.)

C. F. KEIL. *Commentary on the Minor Prophets.* (T. & T. Clark, Edinburgh, 1868.)

W. KELLY. *Lectures Introductory to the Minor Prophets.* (W. H. Broom & Rouse, London, 1897.)

J. KIMCHI. *Commentary on the Prophecies of Zechariah.* (James Duncan, London, 1837.)

T. LAETSCH. *The Minor Prophets.* (Concordia Publishing House, St. Louis, 1956.)

J. P. LANGE. *The Minor Prophets.* (Zondervan Publishing Hous Grand Rapids, n.d.)

H. C. LEUPOLD. *Exposition of Zechariah.* (Wartburg Press, Columbus, 1956.)

W. H. LOWE. *Hebrew Student's Commentary on Zechariah.*

A. MACLAREN. *Ezekiel–Malachi.* (Hodder & Stoughton Ltd., London, n.d.)

T. V. MOORE. *Zechariah.* (Banner of Truth Trust, London, 1968.)

G. CAMPBELL MORGAN. *The Minor Prophets.* (Hodder & Stoughton Ltd., London, n.d.)

W. NEWCOMBE. *Twelve Minor Prophets.* (1809.)

T. T. PEROWNE. *Haggai and Zechariah.* (Cambridge University Press, Cambridge, 1886.)

E. B. PUSEY. *The Minor Prophets.* (Baker Book House, Grand Rapids, 1958.)

J. SKINNER. *The Book of the Prophet Isaiah.* (Cambridge University Press, Cambridge, 1902.)

G. A. SMITH. *The Book of the Twelve Prophets.* (Hodder & Stoughton Ltd., London, 1905.)

F. A. TATFORD. *God's Programme of the Ages.* (Kregel Publications, Grand Rapids, 1967.)

The Prince of Darkness. (B.A.T.M., Eastbourne, 1966.)

Will there be a Millennium? (P.W.P.H., Eastbourne, 1969.)

M. F. UNGER. *Commentary on Zechariah.* (Zondervan Publishing House, Grand Rapids, 1963.)

C. VON ORELLI. *On the Twelve Minor Prophets.* (1893.)

C. H. H. WRIGHT. *Zechariah and His Prophecies.* (E. P. Dutton, New York, 1879.)

J. S. WRIGHT. Article on 'Zechariah' in *New Bible Dictionary.* (Inter Varsity Press, London, 1962.)

W. A. WRIGHT. 'Zechariah' in *A Dictionary of the Bible*, by W. Smith. (John Murray, London, 1863.)